Poetry from 1660 to 1780

Civil War, Restoration, Revolution

Edited by Duncan Wu

based on
*British Literature
1640–1789: An Anthology*

edited by Robert DeMaria Jr

Blackwell
Publishing

Copyright © 2002 by Blackwell Publishers Ltd
a Blackwell Publishing company

Editorial matter, selection and arrangement copyright © Duncan Wu and Robert
DeMaria Jr 2002

Editorial Offices:
108 Cowley Road, Oxford OX4 1JF, UK
Tel: +44 (0)1865 791100
350 Main Street, Malden, MA 02148-5018, USA
Tel: +1 781 388 8250

The Blackwell Publishing logo is a trade mark of Blackwell Publishing Ltd.

First published 2002 by Blackwell Publishers Ltd.

Library of Congress Cataloging-in-Publication Data

Poetry from 1660 to 1780 : Civil War, restoration, revolution / edited by
Duncan Wu.
p. cm.
Includes bibliographical references and index.
ISBN 0-631-22981-7 (alk. paper)—ISBN 0-631-22982-5 (pbk. : alk. paper)
1. English poetry—18th century. 2. English poetry—Early modern, 1500-1700.
I. Wu, Duncan. II. British literature 1640-1789.
PR1217 .P66 2002   821'.509—dc21   2002023953

A catalogue record for this title is available from the British Library

Set in 8/10pt Galliard
by Kolam Information Services Pvt. Ltd, Pondicherry, India
Printed and bound at T.J. International Ltd, Padstow, Cornwall

For further information on
Blackwell Publishers, visit our website:
www.blackwellpublishers.com

Contents

Series Editor's Preface

The Blackwell Essential Literature series offers readers the chance to possess authoritative texts of key poems (and in one case drama) across the standard periods and movements. Based on correspondent volumes in the Blackwell Anthologies series, most of these volumes run to no more than 200 pages. The acknowledged virtues of the Blackwell Anthologies are range and variety; those of the Essential Literature series are authoritative selection, compactness and ease of use. They will be particularly helpful to students hard-pressed for time, who need a digest of the poetry of each historical period.

In selecting the contents of each volume particular attention has been given to major writers whose works are widely taught at most schools and universities. Each volume contains a general introduction designed to introduce the reader to those central works.

Together, these volumes comprise a crucial resource for anyone who reads or studies poetry.

Duncan Wu
St Catherine's College, Oxford

Introduction

Duncan Wu

'The King, in a most rich embroidered suit and cloak, looked most nobly', wrote Samuel Pepys in his diary on 22 April 1661. 'So glorious was the show with gold and silver that we were not able to look at it, our eyes at last being so much overcome with it.' It was an appropriately lavish beginning to a new chapter in English history, concluding the interregnum that followed the civil war and execution of Charles II's father. But that didn't conclude the turmoil begun by Charles I's refusal to bow to the wishes of parliament. In 1688 Charles II's Catholic brother, James II, fled to the Continent, opening the way for a new monarch from Holland, William of Orange, more sympathetic to the notion of a constitutional monarchy subject in some degree to the will of those over whom he ruled.

John Milton had been deeply implicated in the civil war and its aftermath, being among other things Cromwell's Latin secretary. Indeed, at the Restoration Milton was among those arrested and imprisoned, but he narrowly escaped execution and survived to dictate *Paradise Lost* to his amanuenses, of which the first two books are included here. Recent scholarship has emphasized how it is at once a sublime prophetic work, a Protestant poem and an act of political protest. The opening passage beginning 'Of Man's First Disobedience' announces its author's desire to explain how evil came into the world, and why the serpent was in Eden in the first place. In order to do this it was necessary for Milton to invent a myth that could precede the details provided by the Bible, which offered no such explanation. He set the first two books in Hell. During their course we learn that Satan is an emissary from there, a declared enemy of God intent on the destruction of the earth and the appropriation of the pinnacle of God's creation, humankind. Satan, the chief protagonist of these two books, is so convincingly drawn that William Blake was moved to suggest that Milton was of the devil's party without knowing it.[1] It is an ingenious case that has had many adherents, including Shelley and Empson, but Milton would have disagreed. On the surface, Satan is an attractive character; he is a skilful politician and courageous military leader – witty, rhetorically able, even heroic. In leading the fallen angels he is a kind of revolutionary with whom, at a certain level, Milton doubtless sympathized. But there is equivocation in Milton's attitude from the start. The description of Satan sitting in state on his throne in Pandemonium at the start of

---

[1]   William Blake, *The Marriage of Heaven and Hell* (1790), Plate 6.

Book II is laden with references to exotic eastern empires designed to impress. But Milton distrusted monarchs, having written pamphlets in support of Charles I's execution. And Satan's insistence that the fallen angels 'now return / To claim our just inheritance of old' is not revolutionary talk; it is the language of a tyrant. The bizarre allegorical episode of the birth of Sin and Death is designed to bring our attitudes towards him into sharp focus. Rape, incest, intense pain, and violence are the chief features of this horrific tale, and tell us much about the true nature of this most attractive of villains.[2]

Where Milton in his greatest poem is something of a recluse, immersed in myth and religion,[3] John Dryden was the opposite: he identified himself with official opinion and was in some ways the chronicler of his time, capable of writing an elegy on Cromwell and two years later celebrating the return of Charles II in *Astraea Redux*. His conversion to Catholicism coincided with James II's attempts to Catholicize the country – although most commentators, with Auden, take the view that this was not 'a worldly act, but perfectly genuine'.[4] Be this as it may, Dryden was an ambitious, public man, in life as in his poetry, and as such his perspective is necessarily distinct from that of the republican Milton (with whom he had worked in the same government office under Cromwell). Indeed, it is reported that Dryden's political satire *Absalom and Achitophel* (1681) was commissioned by Charles II (whose laureate he had become in 1668). This remarkable poem concerns the so-called 'Exclusion Crisis' of the late 1670s and early 1680s. As Charles II had no legitimate offspring, the largely Protestant Whig party was anxious about his Catholic brother's succession. Rather than allow it, the Earl of Shaftesbury encouraged the Duke of Monmouth (Charles II's illegitimate son) to seize power. That attempt was a failure. In order to relate the history of this abortive enterprise Dryden invokes the biblical story of the rebellion against David, King of Israel, by his son Absalom and his counsellor, Ahithophel the Gilonite. Absalom was Monmouth, King David was Charles II, Ahithophel was Shaftesbury, the Jews were the English, Jerusalem was London, and the Ark of the Covenant was the institution of monarchy, God's special sign of favour towards his chosen race. But in the background Dryden was recalling *Paradise Lost*; Shaftesbury is a fallen Satan (Achitophel), and the youthful and handsome Duke of Monmouth (Absalom) is Adam, tempted to rebel against his father, Charles II, and displace the rightful heir to the throne, James II. In contrast to *Paradise Lost*, however, Dryden's poem is designed to ratify kingship rather

---

[2]   For more on Milton's portrayal of Satan see David Loewenstein, *Milton: Paradise Lost* (Cambridge: Cambridge University Press, 1993), pp. 58–70; David Norbrook, *Writing the English Republic: Poetry, Rhetoric and Politics, 1627–1660* (Cambridge: Cambridge University Press, 1999), pp. 444ff.; John Carey, 'Milton's Satan' in *The Cambridge Companion to Milton* ed. Dennis Danielson (Cambridge: Cambridge University Press, 1989), pp. 131–46.

[3]   Something of a puritan republican himself, Wordsworth was to write of Milton: 'Thy soul was like a Star and dwelt apart' ('Milton! Thou should'st be living at this hour', l. 9).

[4]   *A Choice of Dryden's Verse* selected by W. H. Auden (London: Faber, 1973), p. 8.

than attack it; its subtext is that as the king is anointed by God, rebellion is an act of disobedience towards God. This was precisely the kind of argument that Charles II would have wished his laureate to make.

John Wilmot, Second Earl of Rochester, has been described as 'a realist, his world bounded by the limits of King Charles II's court and the London that lay immediately beyond'.[5] In recent years his work has attracted the interest of many scholars and critics, and several new editions of his works have been produced in the last decade.[6] Those poems presented here are among his best, and show him writing in a range of different voices. 'The Imperfect Enjoyment' ends as a curse poem, in which the speaker rages in mock-heroic manner against his prematurely ejaculating penis; the cynical rake of 'The Disabled Debauchee' dispenses advice to his successors on lustful adventuring; the voice of 'Signior Dildo' is that of the political satirist, as the poet ridicules the importation of the continental helpmeet, and its advocacy by women of the court associated with the Duke of York (it is rejected by those associated with the king); in 'A Letter from Artemiza' Rochester writes in the persona of a female poet who attacks women who take fools for lovers in return for money; that message is reiterated in 'A Ramble in Saint James's Parke' where the maddened speaker relates his betrayal by Corinna, who has rejected him out of fashion. In some ways his most powerful work is 'A Satyr against Reason and Mankind', perhaps because it is here we feel him to be writing as himself. Even here, he is interrupted by a moderating figure of civic authority dismayed by his enraged and relentless assault on reason.

Jonathan Swift is usually read for Gulliver's *Travels* (1726), but he is represented here by, *inter alia*, his scatological poems: 'Strephon and Chloe', 'The Lady's Dressing Room', 'A Beautiful Young Nymph Going to Bed' and 'Cassinus and Peter'. They have been the focus of much critical attention, all preoccupied in various ways with the realities of the human condition. Recent feminist critics, in particular, have been intrigued by the way in which they liberate women from male-constructed fictions of feminine beauty.[7] But 'Verses on the Death of Dr Swift, D.S.P.D.' must be his most accomplished poetical work, as Edward Said has argued:

In that magnificent poem he chooses courageously, even arrogantly, to see himself in the entirely negative aspect of his own death, at once a loss to the world and a gain for history – but in either case an exemplary *subject*. This

---

[5] Barbara Everett, 'Rochester: The Sense of Nothing' in *Poets in their Time: Essays on English Poetry from Donne to Larkin* (London: Faber, 1986), pp. 88–119.

[6] Recent editions include those by David Vieth (1968), Paddy Lyons (1993), Frank Ellis (1994) and Harold Love (1999).

[7] See for example the essays by Carol Houlihan Flynn, Penelope Wilson and Margaret Anne Doody in *Jonathan Swift* ed. Nigel Wood (Harlow: Longman, 1999). A useful reading of the scatological poems may also be found in David Nokes, *Jonathan Swift: A Hypocrite Reversed* (Oxford: Oxford University Press, 1987), pp. 365–72. Psychoanalytical critics have also commented helpfully on these works; see especially Norman O. Brown, *Life Against Death: The Psychoanalytical Meaning of History* (2nd edn Middletown, CT: Wesleyan University Press 1985), pp. 179ff.

summational fiction of his own death is made to take place in the course of the poem as fragmentary responses to a loss being transformed into an event. Thus Swift could become a part of history and a master of it despite the misfortunes attributed by him to language.[8]

Swift's scatological poems might prompt us to wonder how he regarded women. Alexander Pope's *Epistle to a Lady*, with its famous opening couplet ('Nothing so true as what you once let fall, / "Most Women have no Characters at all"'), has helped feed the view that its author was a misogynist. In fact, his early works, 'Epistle to Miss Blount, with the Works of Voiture', *The Rape of the Lock*, 'Eloisa to Abelard' and 'Elegy to the Memory of an Unfortunate Lady', reveal him to have been sympathetic to the plight of women in early eighteenth-century society. He was not alone. In a paper for the *Tatler* in 1710 Richard Steele had deplored the imprisonment of women in loveless marriages.[9] Pope cannot resolve the dilemmas facing women of his time, but his analysis offers compassion and a philosophical insight into how women may best survive in an unjust world. It is most eloquently articulated by Clarissa, whose speech was added to the 1717 text of the *Rape*:

> Since painted, or not painted, all shall fade,
> And she who scorns a man must die a maid;
> What then remains, but well our power to use,
> And keep good-humour still, whate'er we lose? (v. 27–30)

The Rape of the Lock is Pope's masterpiece and deploys the mock-heroic as a means of showing how a trivial incident is turned by its victim into a crime on the same level as the abduction of Helen of Troy. Pope's insight is that this over-reaction is the result, in part, of sexual repression. At the moment prior to the 'rape' he reveals that the protecting influence of the sylphs is short-circuited by the fact that 'An earthly lover' lurks at Belinda's heart. The society in which she lives imposes a marriage market alien from real human relationships, which offers women little more than the sterile pleasures of gracing the front box at the theatre. It is a world in which men and women are compelled to deny or repress their deepest feelings. No wonder, when we descend into the Cave of Spleen, we find such disturbing examples of hysterical behaviour in members of both sexes:

> Here sighs a jar, and there a goose-pie talks:
> Men prove with child, as powerful fancy works,
> And maids turn'd bottles call aloud for corks. (iv. 52–4)

What Clarissa offers, therefore, is rather important. That she has been instrumental in the unfolding drama, having handed the Baron the 'two-

---

[8]   'Swift's Tory Anarchy' in Wood, *Jonathan Swift*, p. 38.
[9]   *Tatler* 149 (21–3 March 1710).

edged weapon' with which he commits the offending act, is significant in itself, in so far as it demonstrates her desire to cut through the hypocrisy of the world in which she lives. The implication is that her role in the 'rape' is part of an educative process – a lesson whereby Belinda is compelled to realize that she has been complicit in what happens. Ariel is rendered powerless to defend her precisely because of the unconscious recognition on Belinda's part that she is in love: 'Amazed, confused, he found his power expired, / Resign'd to fate, and with a sigh retired' (iii. 145–6).

At this early point in his career Pope possessed an acute understanding of human psychology, which emerges in 'Eloisa to Abelard', where sexual frustration is again his theme. The poem is a sort of dramatic monologue by Eloisa, years after her affair with Peter Abelard, which took place when she was sixteen and he in his thirties. He had been her tutor, but they had fallen in love and she had become pregnant. Although they were married in secret, Eloisa denied this to her uncle Fulbert, who assumed that having got her pregnant Abelard wanted to be rid of her. As revenge Fulbert hired two thugs who broke into Abelard's lodgings at night and cut off his genitals. Soon after, Eloisa became a Benedictine nun and Abelard a monk. Now it is impossible for her to free herself of the great passion of her life, and it has become confused with her religious feelings: 'Thy image steals between my God and me' (l. 268). That confusion means that her intense religiosity is found to have a source in her passionate love for Abelard: 'Ev'n here, where frozen chastity retires, / Love finds an altar for forbidden fires' (ll. 181–2).

Samuel Johnson disliked Swift and Pope's satirical writing, but in 'The Vanity of Human Wishes' (1749) he attempts satire in the Juvenalian manner. T. S. Eliot described the result as '*purer* satire than anything of Dryden and Pope, nearer in spirit to the Latin'. Its ambitions are consistent with Imlac's remark to Rasselas in Johnson's novel: 'Human life is every where a state in which much is to be endured, and little to be enjoyed'. The various personages described in the poem are occasionally deluded, misguided, and at the very least not in control of the forces that impel them, often at the cost of their own destruction. Johnson's final message is a moral one: we must find celestial wisdom and accept its calming influence.

It would not be hard to argue the case that Thomas Gray was a failed academic, his ambitions for a history of poetry having run into the sand by the time he became Regius Professor of Modern History, in which capacity he gave no lectures. During his lifetime he published only 14 poems, but among them were some of the greatest of the century, not least 'Ode on a Distant Prospect of Eton College' (1747), 'Ode on the Death of a Favourite Cat' (1748) and 'Elegy Written in a Country Church Yard' (1751). Of these, the 'Elegy' is his most enduring achievement, particularly in its evocation of a ruminative mood. Its portrait of the youth whose death is its occasion would exercise a potent influence on the Romantic perception of the doomed poet:[10]

> There at the foot of yonder nodding beech
> That wreathes its old fantastic roots so high,
> His listless length at noontide would he stretch,
> And pore upon the brook that babbles by. (ll. 101–4)

If this was a success for its impact on the poets who were to follow, William Collins's 'Ode to Evening' was even more influential. The idea of evening as a border moment that connects the earthbound poet to other worlds, other ways of thinking and feeling, had occurred in poetry before, and in some respects recalls Milton's *Il Penseroso*. The distinctive skill of Collins's poem lies in the way in which personification is manipulated to create mood; although the Romantics were to repudiate the eighteenth-century use of personification, they would always admire Collins's sensitivity to tone and atmosphere. Of his contemporaries, Oliver Goldsmith looks forward strongly to what was to come. 'The Deserted Village' is a protest against the depopulation of the countryside by rural landowners, attacking commerce and 'luxury'. It is based, as Goldsmith attested, on direct observation during 'country excursions'. It is innovatory also in its adoption of a meditative manner, in which the poet's own childhood plays its part in bringing Auburn back to life. Wordsworth could not have written 'The Ruined Cottage' without it.[11]

I am much indebted to Robert DeMaria Jr in what follows, and anyone with a serious interest in this poetry should turn to his anthology, listed below, for fuller scholarly treatment.

Further Reading

Corns, Thomas N. (ed.) (2001) *A Companion to Milton* (Oxford: Blackwell).

DeMaria, Robert, Jr (ed.) (1999) *British Literature 1640–1789: A Critical Reader* (Oxford: Blackwell).

DeMaria, Robert, Jr (ed.) (2001) *British Literature 1640–1789: An Anthology*, 2nd edn (Oxford: Blackwell).

Fairer, David and Gerrard, Christine (1999) *Eighteenth-Century Poetry: An Annotated Anthology* (Oxford: Blackwell).

Womersley, David (ed.) (2000) *A Companion to Literature from Milton to Blake* (Oxford: Blackwell).

---

[10]   Gray's influence on the Romantics is discussed by Vincent Newey and some of the other contributors to *Thomas Gray: Contemporary Essays* ed. W. B. Hutchings and William Ruddick (Liverpool: Liverpool University Press, 1993).

[11]   The connection is explored by Jonathan Wordsworth, *The Music of Humanity* (London: Nelson, 1969), pp. 89–91.

John Milton
(1608–1674)

Paradise Lost Book I

The Argument

This first Book proposes, first in brief, the whole Subject, *Man's disobedience, and the loss thereupon of Paradise wherein he was placed:* Then touches *the prime cause of his fall, the Serpent, or rather Satan in the Serpent; who revolting from God, and drawing to his side many Legions of Angels, was by the command of God driven out of Heaven with all his Crew into the great Deep.* Which action passed over, the Poem hastes into the midst of things, presenting *Satan with his Angels now fallen into Hell, described* here, *not in the Centre* (for Heaven and Earth may be supposed as yet not made, certainly not yet accursed) *but in a place of utter darkness, fitliest called Chaos: Here Satan with his Angels lying on the burning Lake, thunder-struck and astonished, after a certain space recovers, as from confusion, calls up him who next in Order and Dignity lay by him; they confer of their miserable fall. Satan awakens all his Legions, who lay till then in the same manner confounded; They rise, their Numbers, array of Battle, their chief Leaders named, according to the Idols known afterwards in Canaan and the Countries adjoining. To these Satan directs his Speech, comforts them with hope yet of regaining Heaven, but tells them lastly of a new World and new kind of Creature to be created, according to an ancient Prophesy or report in Heaven;* for that Angels were long before this visible Creation, was the opinion of many ancient Fathers. *To find out the truth of this Prophesy, and what to determine thereon he refers to a full Council. What his Associates thence attempt.* Pandemonium *the Palace of Satan rises, suddenly built out of the Deep: The infernal Peers there sit in Council.*

> Of Man's First Disobedience, and the Fruit
> Of that Forbidden Tree whose mortal taste
> Brought Death into the World, and all our woe,
> With loss of *Eden*, till one greater Man
> Restore us, and regain the blissful Seat,   5
> Sing, Heav'nly Muse, that on the secret top
> Of *Oreb*, or of *Sinai*, didst inspire
> That Shepherd, who first taught the chosen Seed,
> In the Beginning how the Heav'ns and Earth
> Rose out of *Chaos*: or, if *Sion* hill   10

Delight thee more, and *Siloa*'s Brook that flowed
Fast by the Oracle of God; I thence
Invoke thy aid to my adventrous Song,
That with no middle flight intends to soar
Above th' *Aonian* Mount, while it pursues   15
Things unattempted yet in Prose or Rhyme.
And chiefly Thou, O Spirit, that dost prefer
Before all Temples th' upright heart and pure,
Instruct me, for Thou know'st; Thou from the first
Wast present, and with mighty wings outspread   20
Dove-like sat'st brooding on the vast Abyss,
And mad'st it pregnant: What in me is dark
Illumine, what is low raise and support;
That to the heighth of this great Argument,
I may assert Eternal Providence,   25
And justify the ways of God to men.
    Say first, for Heav'n hides nothing from thy view,
Nor the deep tract of Hell, say first what cause
Moved our Grand Parents, in that happy State,
Favoured of Heav'n so highly, to fall off   30
From their Creator, and transgress his Will
For one restraint, Lords of the World besides?
Who first seduced them to that foul revolt?
Th' infernal Serpent; he it was, whose guile,
Stirred up with Envy and Revenge, deceived   35
The Mother of Mankind, what time his Pride
Had cast him out from Heav'n, with all his Host
Of Rebel Angels, by whose aid aspiring
To set himself in Glory above his Peers,
He trusted to have equalled the Most High,   40
If he opposed; and with ambitious aim
Against the Throne and Monarchy of God
Raised impious War in Heav'n and Battle proud
With vain attempt. Him the Almighty Power
Hurled headlong flaming from th' Ethereal Sky,   45
With hideous ruin and combustion down
To bottomless perdition, there to dwell
In Adamantine Chains and penal Fire,
Who durst defy th' Omnipotent to Arms.
Nine times the Space that measures Day and Night   50
To mortal men, he with his horrid crew
Lay vanquished, rolling in the fiery Gulf,
Confounded though immortal: But his doom
Reserved him to more wrath; for now the thought
Both of lost happiness and lasting pain   55
Torments him; round he throws his baleful eyes,
That witnessed huge affliction and dismay,
Mixed with obdúrate pride and steadfast hate:

At once as far as Angels ken he views
The dismal Situation waste and wild,   60
A Dungeon horrible, on all sides round
As one great Furnace flamed; yet from those flames
No light, but rather darkness visible
Served only to discover sights of woe,
Regions of sorrow, doleful shades, where peace   65
And rest can never dwell, hope never comes
That comes to all; but torture without end
Still urges, and a fiery Deluge, fed
With ever-burning Sulphur unconsumed.
Such place Eternal Justice has prepared   70
For those rebellious, here their Prison ordained
In utter darkness, and their portion set
As far removed from God and light of Heav'n
As from the Centre thrice to th' utmost Pole.
O how unlike the place from whence they fell!   75
There the companions of his fall, o'erwhelmed
With Floods and Whirlwinds of tempestuous fire,
He soon discerns, and weltering by his side
One next himself in power, and next in crime,
Long after known in *Palestine*, and named   80
Beëlzebub. To whom th' Arch-Enemy,
And thence in Heav'n called Satan, with bold words
Breaking the horrid silence, thus began.
     'If thou beest he; but O how fall'n! how changed
From him, who in the happy Realms of Light   85
Clothed with transcendent brightness didst out-shine
Myriads though bright: If he whom mutual league,
United thoughts and counsels, equal hope
And hazard in the Glorious Enterprise,
Joined with me once, now misery hath joined   90
In equal ruin: into what Pit thou seest
From what height fall'n, so much the stronger proved
He with his Thunder: and till then who knew
The force of those dire Arms? yet not for those,
Nor what the Potent Victor in his rage   95
Can else inflict, do I repent or change,
Though changed in outward lustre; that fixed mind
And high disdain, from sense of injured merit,
That with the mightiest raised me to contend,
And to the fierce contention brought along   100
Innumerable force of Spirits armed
That durst dislike his reign, and, me preferring,
His utmost power with adverse power opposed
In dubious Battle on the Plains of Heav'n,
And shook his throne. What though the field be lost?   105
All is not lost; the unconquerable Will,

And study of revenge, immortal hate,
And courage never to submit or yield:
And what is else not to be overcome?
That Glory never shall his wrath or might   110
Extort from me. To bow and sue for grace
With suppliant knee, and deify his power,
Who from the terror of this Arm so late
Doubted his Empire, that were low indeed,
That were an ignominy and shame beneath   115
This downfall; since by Fate the strength of Gods
And this Empyreal Substance cannot fail,
Since through experience of this great event
In Arms not worse, in foresight much advanced,
We may with more successful hope resolve   120
To wage by force or guile eternal War
Irreconcilable, to our grand Foe,
Who now triúmphs, and in th' excess of joy
Sole reigning holds the Tyranny of Heav'n'.
So spake th' Apostate Angel, though in pain,   125
Vaunting aloud, but racked with deep despair:
And him thus answered soon his bold Compeer.
'O Prince, O Chief of many Thronèd Powers,
That led th' embattled Seraphim to War
Under thy conduct, and in dreadful deeds   130
Fearless, endangered Heaven's perpetual King;
And put to proof his high Supremacy,
Whether upheld by strength, or Chance, or Fate,
Too well I see and rue the dire event,
That with sad overthrow and foul defeat   135
Hath lost us Heav'n, and all this mighty Host
In horrible destruction laid thus low,
As far as Gods and Heav'nly Essences
Can perish: for the mind and spirit remains
Invincible, and vigour soon returns,   140
Though all our Glory extinct, and happy state
Here swallowed up in endless misery.
But what if he our Conqueror, (whom I now
Of force believe Almighty, since no less
Than such could have o'erpowered such force as ours)   145
Have left us this our spirit and strength entire,
Strongly to suffer and support our pains,
That we may so suffice his vengeful ire,
Or do him mightier service as his thralls
By right of War, whate'er his business be   150
Here in the heart of Hell to work in Fire,
Or do his Errands in the gloomy Deep;
What can it then avail though yet we feel
Strength undiminished, or eternal being

To undergo eternal punishment?'   155
Whereto with speedy words th' Arch-Fiend replied.
    'Fall'n Cherub, to be weak is miserable
Doing or Suffering: but of this be sure,
To do aught good never will be our task,
But ever to do ill our sole delight,   160
As being the contrary to his high will
Whom we resist. If then his Providence
Out of our evil seek to bring forth good,
Our labour must be to pervert that end,
And out of good still to find means of evil;   165
Which oft times may succeed, so as perhaps
Shall grieve him, if I fail not, and disturb
His inmost counsels from their destined aim.
But see the angry Victor hath recalled
His Ministers of vengeance and pursuit   170
Back to the Gates of Heav'n: the Sulphurous Hail
Shot after us in storm, o'erblown hath laid
The fiery Surge, that from the Precipice
Of Heav'n received us falling, and the Thunder,
Winged with red Lightning and impetuous rage,   175
Perhaps hath spent his shafts, and ceases now
To bellow through the vast and boundless Deep.
Let us not slip th' occasion, whether scorn,
Or satiate fury yield it from our Foe.
Seest thou yon dreary plain, forlorn and wild,   180
The seat of desolation, void of light,
Save what the glimmering of these livid flames
Casts pale and dreadful? Thither let us tend
From off the tossing of these fiery waves,
There rest, if any rest can harbour there,   185
And reassembling our afflicted Powers,
Consult how we may henceforth most offend
Our Enemy, our own loss how repair,
How overcome this dire Calamity,
What reinforcement we may gain from Hope,   190
If not what resolution from despair'.
    Thus Satan, talking to his nearest Mate
With head up-lift above the wave, and eyes
That sparkling blazed, his other Parts besides
Prone on the Flood, extended long and large   195
Lay floating many a rood, in bulk as huge
As whom the Fables name of monstrous size,
Titanian or *Earthborn*, that warred on *Jove*,
Briareos or *Typhon*, whom the Den
By ancient *Tarsus* held, or that Sea-beast   200
Leviathan, which God of all his works
Created hugest that swim th' Oceanstream:

Him, haply slumbering on the *Norway* foam
The Pilot of some small night-foundered Skiff,
Deeming some Island, oft, as Sea-men tell,   205
With fixèd anchor in his scaly rind
Moors by his side under the Lee, while Night
Invests the Sea, and wishèd Morn delays.
So stretcht out huge in length the Arch-fiend lay
Chained on the burning Lake, nor ever thence   210
Had ris'n, or heaved his head, but that the will
And high permission of all-ruling Heaven
Left him at large to his own dark designs,
That with reiterated crimes he might
Heap on himself damnation, while he sought   215
Evil to others, and enraged might see
How all his malice served but to bring forth
Infinite goodness, grace, and mercy shewn
On Man by him seduct, but on himself
Treble confusion, wrath and vengeance poured.   220
Forthwith upright he rears from off the Pool
His mighty Stature; on each hand the flames
Driv'n backward slope their pointing spires, and rolled
In billows, leave i' th' midst a horrid Vale.
Then with expanded wings he steers his flight   225
Aloft, incumbent on the dusky Air
That felt unusual weight, till on dry Land
He lights, if it were Land that ever burned
With solid, as the Lake with liquid fire;
And such appeared in hue, as when the force   230
Of subterranean wind transports a Hill
Torn from *Pelorus*, or the shattered side
Of thundering *Ætna*, whose combustible
And fuellèd entrails thence conceiving fire,
Sublimed with mineral fury, aid the winds,   235
And leave a singèd bottom all involved
With stench and smoke: Such resting found the sole
Of unblest feet. Him followed his next Mate,
Both glorying to have scaped the *Stygian* flood
As Gods, and by their own recovered strength,   240
Not by the sufferance of supernal Power.
   'Is this the Region, this the Soil, the Clime,'
Said then the lost Arch-angel, 'this the seat
That we must change for Heav'n?, this mournful gloom
For that celestial light? Be it so, since he   245
Who now is Sovereign can dispose and bid
What shall be right: farthest from him is best
Whom reason hath equalled, force hath made supreme
Above his equals. Farewell happy Fields
Where Joy for ever dwells: Hail horrors, hail,   250

Infernal world, and thou profoundest Hell
Receive thy new possessor: one who brings
A mind not to be changed by Place or Time.
The mind is its own place, and in it self
Can make a Heav'n of Hell, a Hell of Heav'n.   255
What matter where, if I be still the same,
And what I should be, all but less than he
Whom Thunder hath made greater? Here at least
We shall be free; th' Almighty hath not built
Here for his envy, will not drive us hence: 260
Here we may reign secure; and, in my choice
To reign is worth ambition, though in Hell:
Better to reign in Hell, than serve in Heav'n.
But wherefore let we then our faithful friends,
Th' associates and copartners of our loss   265
Lie thus astonished on' oblivious Pool,
And call them not to share with us their part
In this unhappy Mansion, or once more
With rallied Arms to try what may be yet
Regained in Heav'n, or what more lost in Hell?'   270
    So *Satan* spake; and him *Beëlzebub*
Thus answered. 'Leader of those Armies bright,
Which but th' Omnipotent none could have foiled,
If once they hear that voice, their liveliest pledge
Of hope in fears and dangers, heard so oft   275
In worst extremes, and on the perilous edge
Of battle, when it raged, in all assaults
Their surest signal, they will soon resume
New courage and revive, though now they lie
Grovelling and prostrate on yon Lake of Fire,   280
As we erewhile, astounded and amazed,
No wonder, fall'n such a pernicious height'.
    He scarce had ceased when the superior Fiend
Was moving toward the shore; his ponderous shield,
Ethereal temper, massy, large and round,   285
Behind him cast; The broad circumference
Hung on his shoulders like the Moon, whose Orb
Through Optic Glass the *Tuscan* Artist views
At Evening, from the top of *Fésole*,
Or in Valdarno, to descry new Lands,   290
Rivers or Mountains in her spotty Globe.
His Spear, to equal which the tallest Pine
Hewn on *Norwegian* hills, to be the Mast
Of some great Ammiral, were but a wand,
He walked with to support uneasy steps   295
Over the burning Marl, not like those steps
On Heaven's Azure, and the torrid Clime
Smote on him sore besides, vaulted with Fire,

Nathless he so endured, till on the Beach
Of that inflamèd sea, he stood, and called   300
His Legions, Angel Forms, who lay entranced
Thick as Autumnal Leaves that strow the Brooks
In *Vallombrosa*, where th' *Etrurian* shades
High overarched imbower; or scattered sedge
Afloat, when with fierce Winds *Orion* armed   305
Hath vexed the Red-Sea Coast, whose waves o'erthrew
Busiris and his *Memphian* Chivalry,
While with perfidious hatred they pursued
The sojourners of Goshen, who beheld
From the safe shore their floating carcases   310
And broken Chariot-Wheels, so thick bestrown
Abject and lost lay these, covering the Flood,
Under amazement of their hideous change.
He called so loud, that all the hollow Deep
Of Hell resounded. 'Princes, Potentates,   315
Warriors, the Flower of Heav'n, once yours, now lost,
If such astonishment as this can seize
Eternal Spirits, or have ye chosen this place
After the toil of Battle to repose
Your wearied virtue, for the ease you find   320
To slumber here, as in the Vales of Heav'n?
Or in this abject posture have ye sworn
To adore the Conqueror, who now beholds
Cherub and Seraph rolling in the flood
With scattered Arms and Ensigns, till anon   325
His swift pursuers from Heav'n-Gates discern
Th' advantage, and descending tread us down
Thus drooping, or with linkèd Thunderbolts
Transfix us to the bottom of this Gulf.
Awake, arise, or be for ever fall'n'.   330
    They heard, and were abashed, and up they sprung
Upon the wing, as when men wont to watch
On duty, sleeping found by whom they dread,
Rouse and bestir themselves ere well awake.
Nor did they not perceive the evil plight   335
In which they were, or the fierce pains not feel;
Yet to their General's voice they soon obeyed
Innumerable. As when the potent Rod
Of *Amram*'s Son in *Egypt*'s evil day
Waved round the Coast, upcalled a pitchy cloud   340
Of *Locusts*, warping on the Eastern Wind,
That o'er the Realm of impious *Pharaoh* hung
Like Night, and darkened all the Land of *Nile*:
So numberless were those bad Angels seen
Hovering on wing under the Cope of Hell   345
'Twixt upper, nether, and surrounding Fires;

Till, as a signal giv'n, th' uplifted Spear
Of their great Sultan waving to direct
Their course, in even balance down they light
On the firm brimstone, and fill all the Plain: 350
A multitude, like which the populous North
Poured never from her frozen loins, to pass
Rhene or the *Danaw*, when her barbarous sons
Came like a deluge on the South, and spread
Beneath *Gibraltar* to the *Libian* sands.   355
Forthwith, from every Squadron and each Band
The Heads and Leaders thither haste where stood
Their great Commander; Godlike shapes, and forms
Excelling human, princely Dignities,
And Powers that erst in Heaven sat on thrones,   360
Though of their Names in heav'nly Records now
Be no memorial, blotted out and razed
By their Rebellion from the Books of Life.
Nor had they yet among the sons of *Eve*
Got them new Names, till wandring o'er the Earth,   365
Through God's high sufferance, for the trial of man,
By falsities and lies the greatest part
Of Mankind they corrupted to forsake
God their Creator, and th' invisible
Glory of him that made them, to transform   370
Oft to the Image of a Brute, adorned
With gay Religions full of Pomp and Gold,
And Devils to adore for Deities:
Then were they known to men by various Names,
And various Idols through the Heathen World.   375
Say, Muse, their Names then known, who first, who last,
Roused from the slumber, on that fiery Couch,
At their great Emperor's call, as next in worth
Came singly where he stood on the bare strand,
While the promiscuous crowd stood yet aloof?   380
The chief were those who from the Pit of Hell
Roaming to seek their prey on earth, durst fix
Their Seats long after next the Seat of God,
Their Altars by his Altar, Gods adored
Among the Nations round, and durst abide   385
Jehovah thundering out of *Sion*, throned
Between the Cherubim; yea, often placed
Within his Sanctuary it self their Shrines,
Abominations; and with cursèd things
His holy Rites, and solemn Feasts profaned,   390
And with their darkness durst affront his light.
First *Moloch*, horrid King besmeared with blood
Of human sacrifice, and parents' tears,
Though for the noise of Drums and Timbrels loud,

Their children's cries unheard, that past through fire   395
To his grim Idol. Him the *Ammonite*
Worshipped in *Rabba* and her wat'ry Plain,
In *Argob* and in *Basan*, to the stream
Of utmost *Arnon*. Nor content with such
Audacious neighbourhood, the wisest heart   400
Of *Solomon* he led by fraud to build
His Temple right against the Temple of God
On that opprobrious Hill, and made his Grove
The Pleasant valley of *Hinnom*, *Tophet* thence
And black *Gehenna* called, the Type of Hell.   405
Next *Chemos*, th' obscene dread of *Moab*'s sons,
From *Aroar* to *Nebo*, and the wild
Of Southmost *Abarim*; in *Hesebon*
And *Horonaim*, *Seon*'s realm, beyond
The flowry Dale of *Sibma* clad with Vines,   410
And *Eleale* to th' *Asphaltic* Pool.
Peor his other name, when he enticed
Israel in *Sittim*, on their march from Nile,
To do him wanton rites, which cost them woe.
Yet thence his lustful Orgies he enlarged   415
Even to that Hill of Scandal, by the Grove
Of *Moloch* homicide, lust hard by hate;
Till good *Josiah* drove them thence to Hell.
With these came they, who, from the bordring flood
Of old *Euphrates* to the Brook that parts   420
Egypt from *Syrian* ground, had general Names
Of *Baalim* and *Ashtaroth*, those male,
These Feminine. For Spirits when they please
Can either Sex assume, or both; so soft
And uncompounded is their Essence pure,   425
Not tied or manacled with joint or limb,
Nor founded on the brittle strength of bones,
Like cumbrous flesh; but in what shape they choose
Dilated or condensed, bright or obscure,
Can execute their airy purposes,   430
And works of love or enmity fulfil.
For those the Race of Israel oft forsook
Their living strength, and unfrequented left
His righteous Altar, bowing lowly down
To bestial gods; for which their heads as low   435
Bowed down in Battle, sunk before the Spear
Of despicable foes. With these in troop
Came *Astoreth*, whom the *Phoenicians* called
Astarte, Queen of Heav'n, with crescent Horns;
To whose bright Image nightly by the moon   440
Sidonian virgins paid their Vows and Songs;
In *Sion* also not unsung, where stood

Her Temple on th' offensive Mountain, built
By that uxorious King, whose heart though large,
Beguil'd by fair Idolatresses, fell   445
To Idols foul. *Thammuz* came next behind,
Whose annual wound in *Lebanon* allured
The *Syrian* Damsels to lament his fate
In amorous ditties all a Summer's day,
While smooth *Adonis* from his native Rock   450
Ran purple to the Sea, supposed with blood
Of *Thammuz* yearly wounded: the Love-tale
Infected Sion's daughters with like heat,
Whose wanton passions in the sacred Porch
Ezekiel saw, when by the Vision led   455
His eye surveyed the dark Idolatries
Of alienated *Judah*. Next came one
Who mourned in earnest, when the Captive Ark
Maimed his brute Image, head and hands lopped off
In his own Temple, on the grunsel edge,   460
Where he fell flat, and shamed his Worshippers:
Dagon his Name, Sea Monster, upward Man
And downward Fish; yet had his temple high
Reared in *Azotus*, dreaded, through the Coast
Of *Palestine*, in *Gath* and *Ascalon*,   465
And *Accaron* and *Gaza*'s frontier bounds.
Him followed *Rimmon*, whose delightful Seat
Was fair *Damascus*, on the fertile Banks
Of Abbana and Pharphar, lucid streams.
He also against the house of God was bold: 470
A Leper once he lost and gained a King –
Ahaz his sottish Conqueror, whom he drew
God's Altar to disparage and displace
For one of *Syrian* mode, whereon to burn
His odious offrings, and adore the Gods   475
Whom he had vanquished. After these appeared
A crew who under Names of old Renown –
Osiris, *Isis*, *Orus*, and their Train –
With monstrous shapes and sorceries abused
Fanatic *Egypt* and her Priests, to seek   480
Their wandring Gods disguised in brutish forms
Rather than human. Nor did *Israel* 'scape
Th' infection when their borrowed Gold composed
The Calf in *Oreb*: and the Rebel King
Doubled that sin in *Bethel* and in *Dan*,   485
Lik'ning his Maker to the Grazed Ox,
Jehovah, who in one Night, when he passed
From *Egypt* marching, equalled with one stroke
Both her firstborn and all her bleating Gods.
Belial came last, than whom a Spirit more lewd   490

Fell not from Heav'n, or more gross to love
Vice for itself: to him no Temple stood
Or Altar smoked; yet who more oft than he
In Temples and at Altars, when the Priest
Turns Atheist, as did *Eli*'s Sons, who filled   495
With lust and violence the house of God.
In Courts and Palaces he also Reigns
And in luxurious Cities, where the noise
Of riot ascends above their loftiest Towers,
And injury and outrage: and, when Night   500
Darkens the Streets, then wander forth the Sons
Of *Belial*, flown with insolence and wine.
Witness the Streets of *Sodom*, and that night
In *Gibeah*, when the hospitable door
Exposed a Matron to avoid worse rape.   505
These were the prime in order and in might;
The rest were long to tell, though far renowned
Th' *Ionian* gods – of Javan's issue held
Gods, yet confessed later than Heav'n and Earth,
Their boasted parents; *Titan*, Heav'n's first-born,   510
With his enormous brood, and birthright seized
By younger *Saturn*, he from mightier Jove,
His own and *Rhea*'s son, like measure found;
So *Jove* usurping reigned: these, first in *Crete*
And *Ida* known, thence on the snowy top   515
Of cold Olympus ruled the middle Air,
Their highest Heav'n; or on the *Delphian* Cliff,
Or in Dodona, and through all the bounds
Of *Doric* Land; or who with *Saturn* old
Fled over *Adria* to th' *Hesperian* Fields,   520
And o'er the *Celtic* roamed the utmost Isles.
All these and more came flocking; but with looks
Downcast and damp; yet such wherein appeared
Obscure some glimpse of joy, to have found their chief
Not in despair, to have found themselves not lost   525
In loss itself; which on his countenance cast
Like doubtful hue: but he his wonted pride
Soon recollecting, with high words, that bore
Semblance of worth, not substance, gently raised
Their fainting courage, and dispelled their fears.   530
Then straight commands that, at the warlike sound
Of Trumpets loud and Clarions be upreared
His mighty Standard; that proud honour claimed
Azazel as his right, a Cherub tall:
Who forthwith from the glittering staff unfurled   535
Th' Imperial Ensign, which full high advanced,
Shone like a Meteor streaming to the Wind,
With Gems and Golden lustre rich emblazed,

Seraphic arms and Trophies: all the while
Sonòrous metal blowing martial sounds: 540
At which the universal Host upsent
A shout that tore Hell's Concave, and beyond
Frighted the Reign of *Chaos* and old Night.
All in a moment through the gloom were seen
Ten thousand Banners rise into the Air   545
With Orient Colours waving: with them rose
A Forest huge of Spears: and thronging Helms
Appeared, and serried Shields in thick array
Of depth immeasurable. Anon they move
In perfect Phalanx to the *Dorian* mood   550
Of Flutes and soft Recorders – such as raised
To height of noblest temper Heroes old
Arming to Battle, and in stead of rage
Deliberate valour breathed, firm and unmoved
With dread of death to flight or foul retreat,   555
Nor wanting power to mitigate and swage
With solemn touches, troubled thoughts, and chase
Anguish and doubt and fear and sorrow and pain
From mortal or immortal minds. Thus they,
Breathing united force with fixèd thought   560
Moved on in silence to soft Pipes that charmed
Their painful steps o'er the burnt soil; and now
Advanced in view, they stand, a horrid Front
Of dreadful length and dazzling Arms, in guise
Of Warriors old with ordered Spear and Shield,   565
Awaiting what command their mighty Chief
Had to impose: he through the armèd Files
Darts his experienced eye, and soon traverse
The whole battalion views – their order due,
Their visages and stature as of Gods,   570
Their number last he sums. And now his heart
Distends with pride, and hardning in his strength
Glories: for never since created man,
Met such embodied force as, named with these,
Could merit more than that small infantry   575
Warred on by Cranes: though all the Giant brood
Of *Phlegra* with th' Heroic Race were joined
That fought at *Thebes* and *Ilium*, on each side
Mixed with auxiliar Gods; and what resounds
In Fable or *Romance* of *Uther*'s Son,   580
Begirt with *British* and *Armoric* Knights;
And all who since, Baptized or Infidel,
Jousted in *Aspramont*, or *Montalban*,
Damasco, or *Marocco*, or *Trebisond*,
Or whom *Biserta* sent from *Afric* shore   585
When *Charlémain* with all his Peerage fell

By *Fontarabbia*. Thus far these beyond
Compare of mortal prowess, yet observed
Their dread commander: he, above the rest
In shape and gesture proudly eminent,   590
Stood like a Tower; his form had yet not lost
All her Original brightness, nor appeared
Less than Arch Angel ruined, and th' excess
Of Glory obscured: As when the Sun new ris'n
Looks through the Horizontal misty Air   595
Shorn of his Beams, or from behind the Moon,
In dim Eclipse disastrous twilight sheds
On half the Nations, and with fear of change
Perplexes Monarchs. Darkened so, yet shone
Above them all th' Arch Angel: but his face   600
Deep scars of Thunder had entrenched, and care
Sat on his faded cheek, but under Brows
Of dauntless courage, and considerate Pride
Waiting revenge: cruel his eye, but cast
Signs of remorse and passion, to behold   605
The fellows of his crime, the followers rather
(Far other once beheld in bliss), condemned
For ever now to have their lot in pain –
Millions of Spirits for his fault amerced
Of Heav'n, and from Eternal Splendours flung   610
For his revolt, yet faithful how they stood,
Their Glory withered; as, when Heaven's fire
Hath scathed the Forest Oaks, or Mountain Pines,
With singèd top their stately growth though bare
Stands on the blasted Heath. He now prepared   615
To speak; whereat their doubled Ranks they bend
From wing to wing, and half enclose him round
With all his Peers: attention held them mute.
Thrice he assayed, and thrice in spite of scorn,
Tears such as Angels weep, burst forth: at last   620
Words interwove with sighs found out their way:
  'O Myriads of immortal Spirits, O Powers
Matchless, but with th' Almighty, and that strife
Was not inglorious, though th' event was dire,
As this place testifies, and this dire change,   625
Hateful to utter: but what power of mind
Forseeing or presaging, from the Depth
Of knowledge past or present, could have feared
How such united force of Gods, how such
As stood like these, could ever know repulse?   630
For who can yet believe, though after loss,
That all these puissant Legions, whose exile
Hath emptied Heav'n, shall fail to re-ascend
Self-raised, and repossess their native seat?

For me be witness all the Host of Heav'n,   635
If counsels different, or danger shunned
By me, have lost our hopes. But he who reigns
Monarch in Heav'n till then as one secure
Sat on his Throne, upheld by old repute,
Consent or custom, and his Regal State   640
Put forth at full, but still his strength concealed,
Which tempted our attempt, and wrought our fall.
Henceforth his might we know, and know our own
So as not either to provoke, or dread
New war, provoked; our better part remains   645
To work in close design, by fraud or guile
What force effected not: that he no less
At length from us may find, who overcomes
By force, hath overcome but half his foe.
Space may produce new Worlds; whereof so rife   650
There went a fame in Heav'n that he ere long
Intended to create, and therein plant
A generation, whom his choice regard
Should favour equal to the Sons of Heav'n:
Thither, if but to pry, shall be perhaps   655
Our first eruption, thither, or elsewhere:
For this Infernal Pit shall never hold
Celestial Spirits in Bondage, nor th' Abyss
Long under darkness cover. But these thoughts
Full Counsel must mature: Peace is despaired,   660
For who can think Submission? War then, War
Open or understood must be resolved'.
    He spake: and, to confirm his words, out-flew
Millions of flaming swords, drawn from the thighs
Of mighty Cherubim; the sudden blaze   665
Far round illumined hell: highly they raged
Against the Highest, and fierce with grasped Arms
Clashed on their sounding Shields the din of war,
Hurling defiance toward the Vault of Heav'n.
    There stood a Hill not far whose grisly top   670
Belched fire and rolling smoke; the rest entire
Shone with a glossy scurf, undoubted sign
That in his womb was hid metallic Ore,
The work of Sulphur. Thither winged with speed
A numerous Brigade hastened. As when Bands   675
Of Pioneers with Spade and Pickaxe armed
Forerun the Royal camp, to trench a Field,
Or cast a Rampart. *Mammon* led them on,
Mammon, the least erected Spirit that fell
From heav'n; for ev'n in heav'n his looks and thoughts   680
Were always downward bent, admiring more
The riches of Heav'n's pavement, trodden Gold,

Than aught divine or holy else enjoyed
In vision beatific: by him first
Men also, and by his suggestion taught,   685
Ransacked the Centre, and with impious hands
Rifled the bowels of their mother Earth
For Treasures better hid. Soon had his crew
Opened into the Hill a spacious wound
And digged out ribs of Gold. Let none admire   690
That riches grow in Hell; that soil may best
Deserve the precious bane. And here let those
Who boast in mortal things, and wondering tell
Of *Babel*, and the works of *Memphian* Kings,
Learn how their greatest Monuments of Fame   695
And Strength and Art are easily outdone
By Spirits reprobate, and in an hour
What in an age they with incessant toil
And hands innumerable scarce perform.
Nigh on the Plain in many cells prepared,   700
That underneath had veins of liquid fire
Sluiced from the Lake, a second multitude
With wondrous Art founded the massy Ore,
Severing each kind, and scummed the Bullion dross:
A third as soon had formed within the ground   705
A various mould, and from the boiling cells
By strange conveyance filled each hollow nook,
As in an Organ from one blast of wind
To many a row of Pipes the soundboard breathes.
Anon out of the earth a Fabric huge   710
Rose like an Exhalation, with the sound
Of Dulcet Symphonies and voices sweet,
Built like a Temple, where Pilasters round
Were set, and Doric pillars overlaid
With Golden Architrave; nor did there want   715
Cornice or Frieze, with bossy Sculptures graven;
The Roof was fretted Gold. Not *Babylon*
Nor great *Alcairo* such magnificence
Equalled in all their glories, to enshrine
Belus or *Sarapis* their Gods, or seat   720
Their Kings, when *Egypt* with *Assyria* strove
In wealth and luxury. Th' ascending pile
Stood fixed her stately height, and straight the doors,
Op'ning their brazen folds discover wide
Within, her ample spaces, o'er the smooth   725
And level pavement: from the archèd roof
Pendant by subtle Magic many a row
Of Starry Lamps and blazing Cressets fed
With Naptha and Asphaltus yielded light
As from a sky. The hasty multitude   730

Admiring entered, and the work some praise
And some the Architect: his hand was known
In Heav'n by many a Towered structure high,
Where Sceptred Angels held their residence,
And sat as Princes, whom the supreme King   735
Exalted to such power, and gave to rule,
Each in his Hierarchy, the Orders bright.
Nor was his name unheard or unadored
In ancient *Greece*; and in *Ausonian* land
Men called him *Mulciber*; and how he fell   740
From Heav'n they fabled, thrown by angry *Jove*
Sheer o'er the Crystal Battlements; from Morn
To Noon he fell, from Noon to dewy Eve,
A Summer's day; and with the setting Sun
Dropt from the Zenith like a falling Star,   745
On *Lemnos*, th' Aegean Isle: thus they relate,
Erring; for he with this rebellious rout
Fell long before; nor aught availed him now
To have built in Heav'n high Towers; nor did he scape
By all his Engines, but was headlong sent,   750
With his industrious crew to build in hell.
Mean while the wingèd Heralds by command
Of Sovereign power, with awful Ceremony
And trumpet's sound, throughout the Host proclaim
A solemn Council forthwith to be held   755
At *Pandæmonium*, the high Capital
Of Satan and his Peers: their summons called
From every Band and squarèd Regiment
By place or choice the worthiest; they anon
With hundreds and with thousands trooping came   760
Attended: all access was thronged, the Gates
And Porches wide, but chief the spacious Hall
(Though like a covered field, where Champions bold
Wont ride in armed, and at the Soldan's chair
Defied the best of *Paynim* chivalry   765
To mortal combat, or career with Lance),
Thick swarmed, both on the ground and in the air,
Brushed with the hiss of rustling wings. As Bees
In spring time, when the Sun with *Taurus* rides,
Pour forth their populous youth about the Hive   770
In clusters; they among fresh dews and flow'rs
Fly to and fro, or on the smoothèd Plank,
The suburb of their Straw-built Citadel,
New rubbed with balm, expatiate and confer
Their State affairs. So thick the airy crowd   775
Swarmed and were straitened; till the Signal given,
Behold a wonder! they but now who seemed
In bigness to surpass Earth's Giant Sons

Now less than smallest Dwarfs, in narrow room
Throng numberless, like that Pygméan Race   780
Beyond the *Indian* Mount; or Faerie Elves,
Whose midnight Revels, by a Forest side
Or Fountain some belated Peasant sees,
Or dreams he sees, while overhead the Moon
Sits Arbitress, and nearer to the Earth   785
Wheels her pale course, they on their mirth and dance
Intent, with jocund Music charm his ear;
At once with joy and fear his heart rebounds.
Thus incorporeal Spirits to smallest forms
Reduced their shapes immense, and were at large,   790
Though without number still amidst the hall
Of that infernal Court. But far within,
And in their own dimensions like themselves,
The great Seraphic Lords and Cherubim
In close recess and secret conclave sat,   795
A thousand Demi-Gods on golden seats,
Frequent and full. After short silence then
And summons read, the great consult began.

Book II

The Argument

The Consultation begun, Satan *debates whether another Battle be to be hazarded for the recovery of Heaven: some advise it, others dissuade: A third proposal is preferred, mentioned before by* Satan, *to search the truth of that Prophesy or Tradition in Heaven concerning another world, and another kind of creature equal or not much inferior to themselves, about this time to be created: Their doubt who shall be sent on this difficult search:* Satan *their chief undertakes alone the voyage, is honoured and applauded. The Council thus ended, the rest betake them several ways and to several employments, as their inclinations lead them, to entertain the time till* Satan *return. He passes on his Journey to Hell Gates, finds them shut, and who sat there to guard them, by whom at length they are opened, and discover to him the great Gulf between Hell and Heaven; with what difficulty be passes through, directed by* Chaos, *the Power of that place, to the sight of this new World which he sought.*

High on a Throne of Royal State, which far
Outshone the wealth of *Ormus* and of *Ind*,
Or where the gorgeous East with richest hand
Show'rs on her Kings *Barbaric* Pearl and Gold,
Satan exalted sat, by merit raised   5
To that bad eminence; and from despair
Thus high uplifted beyond hope, aspires

Beyond thus high, insatiate to pursue
Vain War with Heav'n, and by success untaught
His proud imaginations thus displayed.   10
'Powers and Dominions, Deities of Heav'n,
For since no deep within her gulf can hold
Immortal vigour, though oppressed and fall'n,
I give not Heav'n for lost. From this descent
Celestial virtues rising, will appear   15
More glorious and more dread than from no fall,
And trust themselves to fear no second fate:
Me though just right, and the fixed Laws of Heav'n
Did first create your Leader, next free choice,
With what besides, in Counsel or in Fight,   20
Hath been achieved of merit, yet this loss
Thus far at least recovered, hath much more
Established in a safe unenvied Throne
Yielded with full consent. The happier state
In Heav'n, which follows dignity, might draw   25
Envy from each inferior; but who here
Will envy whom the highest place exposes
Foremost to stand against the Thunderer's aim
Your bulwark, and condemns to greatest share
Of endless pain? where there is then no good   30
For which to strive, no strife can grow up there
From Faction; for none sure will claim in Hell
Precedence, none, whose portion is so small
Of present pain, that with ambitious mind
Will covet more. With this advantage then   35
To union, and firm Faith, and firm accord,
More than can be in Heav'n, we now return
To claim our just inheritance of old,
Surer to prosper than prosperity
Could have assured us; and by what best way,   40
Whether of open War or covert guile,
We now debate; who can advise may speak'.
    He ceased, and next him *Moloc*, Sceptred King
Stood up, the strongest and the fiercest Spirit
That fought in Heav'n; now fiercer by despair: 45
His trust was with th' Eternal to be deemed
Equal in strength, and rather than be less
Cared not to be at all; with that care lost
Went all his fear: of God, or Hell, or worse
He recked not, and these words thereafter spake.   50
    'My sentence is for open War: Of Wiles,
More unexpert, I boast not: them let those
Contrive who need, or when they need, not now.
For while they sit contriving, shall the rest,
Millions that stand in arms, and longing wait   55

The Signal to ascend, sit lingering here
Heav'n's fugitives, and for their dwelling place
Accept this dark opprobrious Den of Shame,
The Prison of his Tyranny who Reigns
By our delay? no, let us rather choose   60
Armed with Hell flames and fury all at once
O'er Heav'n's high Towers to force resistless way,
Turning our tortures into horrid arms
Against the Torturer; when, to meet the noise
Of his Almighty Engine, he shall hear   65
Infernal Thunder, and for Lightning see
Black fire and horror shot with equal rage
Among his Angels; and his Throne itself
Mixed with *Tartárean* Sulphur, and strange fire,
His own invented Torments. But perhaps   70
The way seems difficult and steep to scale
With upright wing against a higher foe.
Let such bethink them, if the sleepy drench
Of that forgetful Lake benumb not still,
That in our proper motion we ascend   75
Up to our native seat: descent and fall
To us is adverse. Who but felt of late
When the fierce Foe hung on our broken Rear
Insulting, and pursued us through the Deep,
With what compulsion and laborious flight   80
We sunk thus low? Th' ascent is easy then;
Th' event is feared; should we again provoke
Our stronger, some worse way his wrath may find
To our destruction: if there be in Hell
Fear to be worse destroyed: what can be worse   85
Than to dwell here, driven out from bliss, condemned
In this abhorrèd deep to utter woe;
Where pain of unextinguishable fire
Must exercise us without hope of end
The Vassals of his anger, when the Scourge   90
Inexorably, and the torturing hour
Calls us to Penance? More destroyed than thus
We should be quite abolished, and expire.
What fear we then? what doubt we to incense
His utmost ire? which to the height enraged,   95
Will either quite consume us, and reduce
To nothing this essential, happier far
Than miserable to have eternal being:
Or if our substance be indeed Divine,
And cannot cease to be, we are at worst   100
On this side nothing; and by proof we feel
Our power sufficient to disturb his Heav'n,
And with perpetual inroads to Alarm,

Though inaccessible, his fatal Throne:
Which if not Victory is yet Revenge'.   105
    He ended frowning, and his look denounced
Desperate revenge, and Battle dangerous
To less than Gods. On th' other side up rose
Belial, in act more graceful and humane;
A fairer person lost not Heav'n; he seemed   110
For dignity composed and high exploit:
But all was false and hollow; though his Tongue
Dropt Manna, and could make the worse appear
The better reason, to perplex and dash
Maturest Counsels: for his thoughts were low;   115
To vice industrious, but to Nobler deeds
Timorous and slothful: yet he pleased the ear,
And with persuasive accent thus began.
    'I should be much for open War, O Peers,
As not behind in hate; if what was urged   120
Main reason to persuade immediate War,
Did not dissuade me most, and seem to cast
Ominous conjecture on the whole success:
When he who most excels in fact of Arms,
In what he counsels and in what excels   125
Mistrustful, grounds his courage on despair
And utter dissolution, as the scope
Of all his aim, after some dire revenge.
First, what Revenge? the Towers of Heav'n are filled
With Armèd watch, that render all access   130
Impregnable; oft on the bordering Deep
Encamp their Legions, or with óbscure wing
Scout far and wide into the Realm of night,
Scorning surprise. Or could we break our way
By force, and at our heels all Hell should rise   135
With blackest Insurrection, to confound
Heav'n's purest Light, yet our great Enemy,
All incorruptible would on his Throne
Sit unpolluted, and th' Ethereal mould
Incapable of stain would soon expel   140
Her mischief, and purge off the baser fire
Victorious. Thus repulsed, our final hope
Is flat despair: we must exasperate
Th' Almighty Victor to spend all his rage,
And that must end us, that must be our cure,   145
To be no more; sad cure; for who would lose,
Though full of pain, this intellectual being,
Those thoughts that wander through Eternity,
To perish rather, swallowed up and lost
In the wide womb of uncreated night,   150
Devoid of sense and motion? and who knows,

Let this be good, whether our angry Foe
Can give it, or will ever? how he can
Is doubtful; that he never will is sure.
Will he, so wise, let loose at once his ire,   155
Belike through impotence, or unaware,
To give his Enemies their wish, and end
Them in his anger, whom his anger saves
To punish endless? 'wherefore cease we then?'
Say they who counsel War, 'we are decreed,   160
Reserved and destined to Eternal woe;
Whatever doing, what can we suffer more,
What can we suffer worse?' is this then worst,
Thus sitting, thus consulting, thus in Arms?
What when we fled amain, pursued and strook   165
With Heav'n's afflicting Thunder, and besought
The Deep to shelter us? this Hell then seemed
A refuge from those wounds: or when we lay
Chained on the burning Lake? that sure was worse.
What if the breath that kindled those grim fires   170
Awaked should blow them into sevenfold rage
And plunge us in the flames? or from above
Should intermitted vengeance arm again
His red right hand to plague us? what if all
Her stores were opened, and this Firmament   175
Of Hell should spout her Cataracts of Fire,
Impendent horrors, threatning hideous fall
One day upon our heads; while we perhaps
Designing or exhorting glorious war,
Caught in a fiery Tempest shall be hurled   180
Each on his rock transfixed, the sport and prey
Or racking whirlwinds, or for ever sunk
Under yon boiling Ocean, wrapped in Chains;
There to converse with everlasting Groans,
Unrespited, unpitied, unreprieved,   185
Ages of hopeless end; this would be worse.
War therefore, open or concealed, alike
My voice dissuades; for what can force or guile
With him, or who deceive his mind, whose eye
Views all things at one view? he from Heav'n's heighth   190
All these our motions vain, sees and derides;
Not more Almighty to resist our might
Than wise to frustrate all our plots and wiles.
Shall we then live thus vile, the race of Heav'n
Thus trampled, thus expelled, to suffer here   195
Chains and these Torments? Better these than worse,
By my advice; since fate inevitable
Subdues us, and Omnipotent Decree,
The Victor's will. To suffer, as to do,

Our strength is equal, nor the Law unjust　　　　　200
That so ordains: this was at first resolved,
If we were wise, against so great a foe
Contending, and so doubtful what might fall.
I laugh when those who at the Spear are bold
And venturous, if that fail them, shrink and fear　　205
What yet they know must follow, to endure
Exile, or ignominy, or bonds, or pain,
The sentence of their Conqueror: This is now
Our doom; which if we can sustain and bear,
Our Súpreme Foe in time may much remit　　　　210
His anger, and perhaps thus far removed
Not mind us not offending, satisfied
With what is punished; whence these raging fires
Will slacken, if his breath stir not their flames.
Our purer essence then will overcome　　　　　215
Their noxious vapour, or inured not feel,
Or changed at length, and to the place conformed
In temper and in nature, will receive
Familiar the fierce heat, and void of pain;
This horror will grow mild, this darkness light,　　220
Besides what hope the never-ending flight
Of future days may bring, what chance, what change
Worth waiting, since our present lot appears
For happy though but ill, for ill not worst,
If we procure not to our selves more woe'.　　　　225
　　Thus *Belial*, with words clothed in reason's garb
Counselled ignoble ease, and peaceful sloth,
Not peace: and after him thus *Mammon* spake.
　　'Either to disenthrone the King of Heav'n
We war, if war be best, or to regain　　　　　230
Our own right lost: him to unthrone we then
May hope when everlasting Fate shall yield
To fickle Chance, and *Chaos* judge the strife:
The former vain to hope argues as vain
The latter: for what place can be for us　　　　235
Within Heav'n's bound, unless Heav'n's Lord supreme
We overpower? Suppose he should relent
And publish Grace to all, on promise made
Of new Subjection; with what eyes could we
Stand in his presence humble, and receive　　　240
Strict Laws imposed, to celebrate his Throne
With warbled Hymns, and to his Godhead sing
Forced Hallelujahs; while he Lordly sits
Our envied Sovereign, and his Altar breathes
Ambrosial Odours and Ambrosial Flowers,　　　245
Our servile offerings. This must be our task
In Heav'n this our delight; how wearisome

Eternity so spent in worship paid
To whom we hate. Let us not then pursue
By force impossible, by leave obtained   250
Unacceptable, though in Heav'n, our state
Of splendid vassalage, but rather seek
Our own good from our selves, and from our own
Live to our selves, though in this vast recess,
Free, and to none accountable, preferring   255
Hard liberty before the easy yoke
Of servile Pomp. Our greatness will appear
Then most conspicuous, when great things of small,
Useful of hurtful, prosperous of adverse
We can create, and in what place soe'er   260
Thrive under evil, and work ease out of pain
Through labour and endurance. This deep world
Of darkness do we dread? How oft amidst
Thick clouds and dark doth Heav'n's all-ruling Sire
Choose to reside, his Glory unobscured,   265
And with the Majesty of darkness round
Covers his Throne; from whence deep thunders roar
Mustering their rage, and Heav'n resembles Hell?
As he our darkness, cannot we his Light
Imitate when we please? This Desert soil   270
Wants not her hidden lustre, Gems and Gold;
Nor want we skill or Art, from whence to raise
Magnificence; and what can Heav'n show more?
Our torments also may in length of time
Become our Elements, these piercing Fires   275
As soft as now severe, our temper changed
Into their temper; which must needs remove
The sensible of pain. All things invite
To peaceful Counsels, and the settled State
Of order, how in safety best we may   280
Compose our present evils, with regard
Of what we are and where, dismissing quite
All thoughts of War: ye have what I advise'.
   He scarce had finished, when such murmur filled
Th' Assembly, as when hollow Rocks retain   285
The sound of blustering winds, which all night long
Had roused the Sea, now with hoarse cadence lull
Sea-faring men o'erwatched, whose Bark by chance
Or Pinnace anchors in a craggy Bay
After the Tempest: Such applause was heard   290
As *Mammon* ended, and his Sentence pleased,
Advising peace: for such another Field
They dreaded worse than Hell; so much the fear
Of Thunder and the Sword of *Michaël*
Wrought still within them; and no less desire   295

To found this nether Empire, which might rise
By policy and long process of time,
In emulation opposite to Heav'n.
Which when *Beëlzebub* perceived, than whom,
Satan except, none higher sat, with grave   300
Aspect he rose, and in his rising seemed
A Pillar of State; deep on his Front engraven
Deliberation sat and public care;
And Princely counsel in his face yet shone,
Majestic though in ruin: *Sage* he stood   305
With *Atlantean* shoulders fit to bear
The weight of mightiest Monarchies; his look
Drew audience and attention still as Night
Or summer's Noon-tide air, while thus he spake.
  'Thrones and Imperial Powers, off-spring of Heav'n   310
Ethereal Virtues; or these Titles now
Must we renounce, and changing style be called
Princes of Hell? for so the popular vote
Inclines, here to continue, and build up here
A growing Empire; doubtless; while we dream,   315
And know not that the King of Heav'n hath doomed
This place our dungeon, not our safe retreat
Beyond his Potent arm, to live exempt
From Heav'n's high jurisdiction, in new League
Banded against his Throne, but to remain   320
In strictest bondage, though thus far removed,
Under th' inevitable curb, reserved
His captive multitude: For he, to be sure
In height or depth, still first and last will Reign
Sole King, and of his Kingdom lose no part   325
By our revolt, but over Hell extend
His Empire, and with Iron Sceptre rule
Us here, as with his Golden those in Heav'n.
What sit we then projecting peace and War?
War hath determined us and foiled with loss   330
Irreparable; terms of peace yet none
Vouchsafed or sought; for what peace will be giv'n
To us enslaved, but custody severe,
And stripes, and arbitrary punishment
Inflicted? and what peace can we return,   335
But to our power hostility and hate,
Untamed reluctance, and revenge though slow,
Yet ever plotting how the Conqueror least
May reap his conquest, and may least rejoice
In doing what we most in suffering feel?   340
Nor will occasion want, nor shall we need
With dangerous expedition to invade
Heav'n, whose high walls fear no assault or Siege,

Or ambush from the Deep. What if we find
Some easier enterprise? There is a place   345
(if ancient and prophetic fame in Heav'n
Err not) another World, the happy seat
Of some new Race called *Man*, about this time
To be created like to us, though less
In power and excellence, but favoured more   350
Of him who rules above; so was his will
Pronounced among the Gods, and by an Oath,
That shook Heav'n's whole circumference, confirmed.
Thither let us bend all our thoughts, to learn
What creatures there inhabit, of what mould,   355
Or substance, how endued, and what their Power,
And where their weakness, how attempted best,
By force or subtlety: Though Heav'n be shut,
And Heav'n's high Arbitrator sit secure
In his own strength, this place may lie exposed   360
The utmost border of his Kingdom, left
To their defence who hold it: here perhaps
Some advantageous act may be achieved
By sudden onset, either with Hell fire
To waste his whole Creation, or possess   365
All as our own, and drive as we were driven,
The puny habitants, or if not drive,
Seduce them to our Party, that their God
May prove their foe, and with repenting hand
Abolish his own works. This would surpass   370
Common revenge, and interrupt his joy
In our Confusion, and our Joy upraise
In his disturbance; when his darling Sons,
Hurled headlong to partake with us, shall curse
Their frail original, and faded bliss,   375
Faded so soon. Advise if this be worth
Attempting, or to sit in darkness here
Hatching vain Empires'. Thus *Beëlzebub*
Pleaded his devilish Counsel, first devised
By *Satan*, and in part proposed: for whence,   380
But from the Author of all ill could Spring
So deep a malice, to confound the race
Of mankind in one root, and Earth with Hell
To mingle and involve, done all to spite
The great Creator? But their spite still serves   385
His glory to augment. The bold design
Pleased highly those infernal States, and joy
Sparkled in all their eyes; with full assent
They vote: whereat his speech he thus renews.
    'Well have ye judged, well ended long debate,   390
Synod of Gods, and like to what ye are,

Great things resolved, which from the lowest deep
Will once more lift us up, in spite of Fate,
Nearer our ancient Seat; perhaps in view
Of those bright confines, whence with neighbouring Arms   395
And opportune excursion we may chance
Re-enter Heav'n; or else in some mild Zone
Dwell not unvisited of Heav'n's fair Light
Secure, and at the brightning Orient beam
Purge off this gloom; the soft delicious Air,   400
To heal the scar of these corrosive Fires
Shall breathe her balm. But first whom shall we send
In search of this new world? whom shall we find
Sufficient? who shall tempt with wandring feet
The dark unbottomed infinite Abyss   405
And through the palpable obscure find out
His uncouth way, or spread his airy flight
Upborn with indefatigable wings
Over the vast abrupt, ere he arrive
The happy Isle; what strength, what art can then   410
Suffice, or what evasion bear him safe
Through the strict Senteries and Stations thick
Of Angels watching round? Here he had need
All circumspection, and we now no less
Choice in our suffrage; for on whom we send,   415
The weight of all and our last hope relies'.
    This said, he sat; and expectation held
His look suspense, awaiting who appeared
To second, or oppose, or undertake
The perilous attempt: but all sat mute,   420
Pondering the danger with deep thoughts; and each
In other's countenance read his own dismay
Astonished: none among the choice and prime
Of those Heav'n-warring Champions could be found
So hardy as to proffer or accept   425
Alone the dreadful voyage; till at last
Satan, whom now transcendent glory raised
Above his fellows, with Monarchal pride
Conscious of highest worth, unmoved thus spake.
    'O Progeny of Heav'n! Empyreal Thrones,   430
With reason hath deep silence and demur
Seized us, though undismayed: long is the way
And hard, that out of Hell leads up to light;
Our prison strong, this huge convex of Fire,
Outrageous to devour, immures us round   435
Ninefold, and gates of burning adamant
Barred over us prohibit all egress.
These past, if any pass, the void profound
Of unessential Night receives him next

Wide gaping, and with utter loss of being   440
Threatens him, plunged in that abortive gulf.
If thence he scape into whatever world,
Or unknown Region, what remains him less
Than unknown dangers and as hard escape.
But I should ill become this Throne, O Peers,   445
And this Imperial sovereignty, adorned
With splendour, armed with power, if aught proposed
And judged of public moment, in the shape
Of difficulty or danger could deter
Me from attempting. Wherefore do I assume   450
These Royalties, and not refuse to Reign,
Refusing to accept as great a share
Of hazard as of honour, due alike
To him who Reigns, and so much to him due
Of hazard more, as he above the rest   455
High honoured sits? Go therefore mighty Powers,
Terror of Heav'n, though fall'n; intend at home,
While here shall be our home, what best may ease
The present misery, and render Hell
More tolerable; if there be cure or charm   460
To respite or deceive, or slack the pain
Of this ill Mansion: intermit no watch
Against a wakeful Foe, while I abroad
Through all the Coasts of dark destruction seek
Deliverance for us all: this enterprise   465
None shall partake with me'. Thus saying rose
The Monarch, and prevented all reply,
Prudent, lest, from his resolution raised
Others among the chief might offer now
(Certain to be refused) what erst they feared;   470
And so refused might in opinion stand
His Rivals, winning cheap the high repute
Which he through hazard huge must earn. But they
Dreaded not more th' adventure than his voice
Forbidding; and at once with him they rose;   475
Their rising all at once was as the sound
Of Thunder heard remote. Towards him they bend
With awful reverence prone; and as a God
Extol him equal to the highest in Heav'n:
Nor failed they to express how much they praised,   480
That for the general safety he despised
His own: for neither do the Spirits damned
Lose all their virtue; lest bad men should boast
Their specious deeds on earth, which glory excites,
Or close ambition varnished o'er with zeal.   485
Thus they their doubtful consultations dark
Ended rejoicing in their matchless Chief:

As when from mountain tops the dusky clouds
Ascending, while the North wind sleeps, o'erspread
Heav'n's cheerful face, the louring element   490
Scowls o'er the darkened lantskip Snow or shower;
If chance the radiant Sun with farewell sweet
Extend his ev'ning beam, the fields revive,
The birds their notes renew, and bleating herds
Attest their joy, that hill and valley rings.   495
O shame to men! Devil with Devil damned
Firm concord holds, men only disagree
Of Creatures rational, though under hope
Of heavenly Grace: and God proclaiming peace,
Yet live in hatred, enmity, and strife   500
Among themselves, and levy cruel wars
Wasting the Earth, each other to destroy:
As if (which might induce us to accord)
Man had not hellish foes enow besides,
That day and night for his destruction wait.   505
    The *Stygian* Counsel thus dissolved; and forth
In order came the grand infernal Peers,
Midst came their mighty Paramount, and seemed
Alone th' Antagonist of Heav'n, nor less
Than Hell's dread Emperor with pomp supreme,   510
And God-like imitated State; him round
A Globe of fiery Seraphim enclosed
With bright emblazonry, and horrent Arms.
Then of their Session ended they bid cry
With Trumpet's regal sound the great result: 515
Toward the four winds four speedy Cherubim
Put to their mouths the sounding Alchemy
By Herald's voice explained: the hollow Abyss
Heard far and wide, and all the host of Hell
With deafning shout, returned them loud acclaim.   520
Thence more at ease their minds and somewhat raised
By false presumptuous hope, the rangèd powers
Disband, and wandring, each his several way
Pursues, as inclination or sad choice
Leads him perplext, where he may likeliest find   525
Truce to his restless thoughts, and entertain
The irksome hours, till his great Chief return.
Part on the Plain, or in the Air sublime
Upon the wing, or in swift Race contend,
As at th' *Olympian* Games or *Pythian* fields;   530
Part curb their fiery Steeds, or shun the Goal
With rapid wheels, or fronted Brígades form.
As when to warn proud Cities war appears
Waged in the troubled Sky, and Armies rush
To Battle in the Clouds, before each Van   535

Prick forth the Airy Knights, and couch their spears
Till thickest Legions close; with feats of Arms
From either end of Heav'n the welkin burns.
Others with vast *Typhoean* rage, more fell
Rend up both Rocks and Hills, and ride the Air   540
In whirlwind; Hell scarce holds the wild uproar.
As when *Alcides* from *Oechalia* Crowned
With conquest, felt th' envenomed robe, and tore
Through pain up by the roots *Thessalian* Pines,
And *Lichas* from the top of *Oeta* threw   545
Into th' *Euboic* Sea. Others more mild,
Retreated in a silent valley, sing
With notes Angelical to many a Harp
Their own Heroic deeds and hapless fall
By doom of battle; and complain that Fate   550
Free Virtue should enthrall to Force or Chance.
Their Song was partial, but the harmony
(What could it less when Spirits immortal sing?)
Suspended Hell, and took with ravishment
The thronging audience. In discourse more sweet   555
(For Eloquence the Soul, Song charms the Sense,)
Others apart sat on a Hill retired,
In thoughts more elevate, and reasoned high
Of Providence, Foreknowledge, Will and Fate,
Fixed fate, free will, foreknowledge absolute,   560
And found no end, in wandring mazes lost.
Of good and evil much they argued then,
Of happiness and final misery,
Passion and Apathy, and glory and shame,
Vain wisdom all, and false Philosophy: 565
Yet with a pleasing sorcery could charm
Pain for a while or anguish, and excite
Fallacious hope, or arm th' obdurèd breast
With stubborn patience as with triple steel.
Another part in Squadrons and gross Bands,   570
On bold adventure to discover wide
That dismal world, if any clime perhaps
Might yield them easier habitation, bend
Four ways their flying March, along the Banks
Of four infernal Rivers that disgorge   575
Into the burning Lake their baleful streams;
Abhorred *Styx* the flood of deadly hate,
Sad *Acheron* of sorrow, black and deep;
Cocytus, named of lamentation loud
Heard on the rueful stream; fierce *Phlegeton*   580
Whose waves of torrent fire inflame with rage.
Far off from these a slow and silent stream,
Lethe the River of Oblivion, rolls

Her wat'ry Labyrinth, whereof who drinks,
Forthwith his former state and being forgets,   585
Forgets both joy and grief, pleasure and pain.
Beyond this flood a frozen continent
Lies dark and wild, beat with perpetual storms
Of Whirlwind and dire Hail, which on firm land
Thaws not, but gathers heap, and ruin seems   590
Of ancient pile; all else deep snow and ice,
A gulf profound as that *Serbonian* bog
Betwixt *Damiata* and mount *Casius* old,
Where Armies whole have sunk: the parching Air
Burns frore, and cold performs th' effect of Fire.   595
Thither by harpy-footed Furies hailed,
At certain revolutions all the damned
Are brought: and feel by turns the bitter change
Of fierce extremes, extremes by change more fierce,
From Beds of raging Fire to starve in Ice   600
Their soft Ethereal warmth, and there to pine
Immovable, infixed, and frozen round,
Periods of time, thence hurried back to fire.
They ferry over this *Lethean* Sound
Both to and fro, their sorrow to augment,   605
And wish and struggle, as they pass, to reach
The tempting stream, with one small drop to lose
In sweet forgetfulness all pain and woe,
All in one moment, and so near the brink;
But Fate withstands, and to oppose th' attempt   610
Medusa with *Gorgonian* terror guards
The Ford, and of itself the water flies
All taste of living wight, as once it fled
The lip of *Tantalus*. Thus roving on
In confused march forlorn, th' adventrous Bands   615
With shuddring horror pale, and eyes aghast
Viewed first their lamentable lot, and found
No rest: through many a dark and dreary Vale
They passed, and many a Region dolorous,
O'er many a Frozen, many a fiery Alp,   620
Rocks, Caves, Lakes, Fens, Bogs, Dens, and shades of death,
A Universe of death, which God by curse
Created evil, for evil only good,
Where all life dies, death lives, and Nature breeds,
Perverse, all monstrous, all prodigious things,   625
Abominable, inutterable, and worse
Than fables yet have feigned, or fear conceived,
Gorgons and *Hydras*, and *Chimeras* dire.
     Meanwhile the Adversary of God and Man,
Satan with thoughts inflamed of highest design,   630
Puts on swift wings, and towards the Gates of Hell

Explores his solitary flight; some times
He scours the right hand coast, sometimes the left,
Now shaves with level wing the Deep, then soars
Up to the fiery Concave towering high.   635
As when far off at Sea a fleet descried
Hangs in the Clouds, by Equinoctial Winds
Close sailing from *Bengala*, or the Isles
Of *Ternate* and *Tidore*, whence Merchants bring
Their spicy Drugs: they on the Trading Flood   640
Through the wide *Ethiopian* to the Cape
Ply stemming nightly toward the Pole. So seemed
Far off the flying Fiend: at last appear
Hell bounds high reaching to the horrid Roof,
And thrice threefold the Gates; three folds were Brass,   645
Three Iron, three of Adamantine Rock,
Impenetrable, impaled with circling fire,
Yet unconsumed. Before the Gates there sat
On either side a formidable shape;
The one seemed Woman to the waist, and fair,   650
But ended foul in many a scaly fold
Voluminous and vast, a Serpent armed
With mortal sting: about her middle round
A cry of Hell Hounds never ceasing barked
With wide *Cerberian* mouths full loud, and rung   655
A hideous Peal: yet, when they list, would creep,
If aught disturbed their noise, into her womb,
And kennel there, yet there still barked and howled,
Within unseen. Far less abhorred than these
Vexed *Scylla* bathing in the Sea that parts   660
Calabria from the hoarse *Trinacrian* shore:
Nor uglier follow the Night-Hag, when called
In secret, riding through the Air she comes
Lured with the smell of infant blood, to dance
With *Lapland* Witches, while the labouring Moon   665
Eclipses at their charms. The other shape,
If shape it might be called that shape had none
Distinguishable in member, joint, or limb,
Or substance might be called that shadow seemed,
For each seemed either; black it stood as Night,   670
Fierce as ten Furies, terrible as Hell,
And shook a dreadful Dart: what seemed his head
The likeness of a Kingly Crown had on.
Satan was now at hand, and from his seat
The Monster moving onward came as fast   675
With horrid strides; Hell trembled as he strode.
Th' undaunted Fiend what this might be admired,
Admired, not feared; God and his Son except,
Created thing naught valued he nor shunned;

And with disdainful look thus first began.   680
    'Whence and what art thou, execrable shape,
That darest, though grim and terrible, advance
Thy miscreated Front athwart my way
To yonder Gates? through them I mean to pass,
That be assured, without leave asked of thee.   685
Retire, or taste thy folly, and learn by proof,
Hell-born, not to contend with Spirits of Heav'n'.
    To whom the Goblin full of wrath, replied,
'Art thou that traitor Angel, art thou he,
Who first broke peace in Heav'n and Faith, till then   690
Unbroken, and in proud rebellious Arms
Drew after him the third part of Heav'n's Sons
Conjured against the Highest, for which both Thou
And they outcast from God, are here condemned
To waste eternal days in woe and pain?   695
And reckonst thou thy self with Spirits of Heav'n,
Hell-doomed, and breathest defiance here and scorn
Where I reign King, and to enrage thee more,
Thy King and Lord? Back to thy punishment,
False fugitive, and to thy speed add wings,   700
Lest with a whip of Scorpions I pursue
Thy lingring, or with one stroke of this Dart
Strange horror seize thee, and pangs unfelt before'.
    So spake the grisly terror, and in shape,
So speaking and so threatning, grew tenfold   705
More dreadful and deform: on th' other side
Incensed with indignation *Satan* stood
Unterrified, and like a Comet burned,
That fires the length of *Ophiucus* huge
In th' arctic sky, and from his horrid hair   710
Shakes pestilence and War. Each at the head
Levelled his deadly aim; their fatal hands
No second stroke intend, and such a frown
Each cast at th' other, as when two black Clouds
With Heav'n's Artillery fraught, come rattling on   715
Over the *Caspian*, then stand front to front
Hovering a space, till winds the signal blow
To join their dark encounter in mid air:
So frowned the mighty Combatants, that Hell
Grew darker at their frown, so matched they stood;   720
For never but once more was either like
To meet so great a foe: and now great deeds
Had been achieved, whereof all Hell had rung,
Had not the snaky Sorceress that sat
Fast by Hell-gate and kept the fatal key,   725
Risen, and with hideous outcry rushed between:
    'O Father, what intends thy hand', she cried,

'Against thy only Son? What fury O Son,
Possesses thee to bend that mortal Dart
Against thy Father's head? and know'st for whom: 730
For him who sits above and laughs the while
At thee ordained his drudge, to execute
What e're his wrath, which he calls Justice, bids,
His wrath which one day will destroy ye both'.

   She spake, and at her words the hellish Pest   735
Forbore, then these to her *Satan* returned:
   'So strange thy outcry, and thy words so strange
Thou interposest, that my sudden hand
Prevented spares to tell thee yet by deeds
What it intends; till first I know of thee,   740
What thing thou art, thus double-formed, and why
In this infernal Vale first met thou call'st
Me father, and that Phantasm call'st my Son?
I know thee not, nor ever saw till now
Sight more detestable than him and thee'.   745

   T' whom thus the Portress of Hell Gate replied;
'Hast thou forgot me then, and do I seem
Now in thine eye so foul, once deemed so fair
In Heav'n, when at th' Assembly, and in sight
Of all the Seraphim with thee combined   750
In bold conspiracy against Heav'n's King,
All on a sudden miserable pain
Surprised thee, dim thine eyes, and dizzy swum
In darkness, while thy head flames thick and fast
Threw forth, till on the left side opening wide,   755
Likest to thee in shape and countenance bright,
Then shining heav'nly fair, a Goddess armed
Out of thy head I sprung. Amazement seized
All th' Host of Heav'n; back they recoiled afraid
At first, and called me *Sin*, and for a Sign   760
Portentous held me; but familiar grown,
I pleased, and with attractive graces won
The most averse, thee chiefly, who full oft
Thy self in me thy perfect image viewing
Becam'st enamoured, and such joy thou took'st   765
With me in secret, that my womb conceived
A growing burden. Meanwhile war arose,
And fields were fought in Heav'n; wherein remained
(For what could else) to our Almighty Foe
Clear victory, to our part loss and rout   770
Through all the Empyrean: down they fell
Driven headlong from the Pitch of Heav'n, down
Into this Deep, and in the general fall
I also; at which time this powerful Key
Into my hands was given, with charge to keep   775

These Gates for ever shut, which none can pass
Without my opening. Pensive here I sat
Alone, but long I sat not, till my womb,
Pregnant by thee, and now excessive grown
Prodigious motion felt and rueful throes.   780
At last this odious offspring whom thou seest
Thine own begotten, breaking violent way
Tore through my entrails, that with fear and pain
Distorted, all my nether shape thus grew
Transformed: but he my inbred enemy   785
Forth issued, brandishing his fatal Dart
Made to destroy: I fled, and cried out *Death*;
Hell trembled at the hideous Name, and sighed
From all her Caves, and back resounded *Death*;
I fled, but he pursued (though more, it seems,   790
Inflamed with lust than rage) and swifter far,
Me overtook his mother all dismayed,
And in embraces forcible and foul
Engendring with me, of that rape begot
These yelling Monsters that with ceaseless cry   795
Surround me, as thou sawst, hourly conceived
And hourly born, with sorrow infinite
To me, for when they list into the womb
That bred them they return, and howl and gnaw
My Bowels, their repast; then bursting forth   800
Afresh with conscious terrors vex me round,
That rest or intermission none I find.
Before mine eyes in opposition sits
Grim *Death* my Son and foe who sets them on,
And me his Parent would full soon devour   805
For want of other prey, but that he knows
His end with mine involved; and knows that I
Should prove a bitter Morsel, and his bane,
Whenever that shall be; so Fate pronounced.
But thou O Father, I forewarn thee, shun   810
His deadly arrow; neither vainly hope
To be invulnerable in those bright Arms,
Though tempered Heav'nly, for that mortal dint,
Save he who reigns above, none can resist'.
    She finished, and the subtle Fiend his lore   815
Soon learned, now milder, and thus answered smooth.
'Dear Daughter, since thou claim'st me for thy Sire,
And my fair Son here showst me, the dear pledge
Of dalliance had with thee in Heav'n, and joys
Then sweet, now sad to mention, through dire change   820
Befallen us unforeseen, unthought of, know
I come no enemy, but to set free
From out this dark and dismal house of pain,

Both him and thee, and all the heav'nly Host
Of Spirits that in our just pretences armed   825
Fell with us from on high: from them I go
This uncouth errand sole, and one for all
My self expose, with lonely steps to tread
Th' unfounded deep, and through the void immense
To search with wandring quest, a place foretold   830
Should be, and, by concurring signs, ere now
Created vast and round, a place of bliss
In the purlieus of Heav'n, and therein placed
A race of upstart Creatures, to supply
Perhaps our vacant room, though more removed,   835
Lest Heav'n, surcharged with potent multitude
Might hap to move new broils: Be this or aught
Than this more secret now designed, I haste
To know, and this once known, shall soon return,
And bring ye to the place where Thou and Death   840
Shall dwell at ease, and up and down unseen
Wing silently the buxom Air, embalmed
With odours; there ye shall be fed and filled
Immeasurably, all things shall be your prey'.
He ceased, for both seemed highly pleased, and Death   845
Grinned horrible a ghastly smile, to hear
His famine should be filled, and blessed his maw
Destined to that good hour: no less rejoiced
His mother bad, and thus bespake her Sire.
   'The key of this infernal Pit by due,   850
And by command of Heav'n's all-powerful King
I keep, by him forbidden to unlock
These Adamantine Gates; against all force
Death ready stands to interpose his dart,
Fearless to be o'ermatched by living might.   855
But what owe I to his commands above
Who hates me, and hath hither thrust me down
Into this gloom of *Tartarus* profound,
To sit in hateful Office here confined,
Inhabitant of Heav'n, and heav'nly-born,   860
Here in perpetual agony and pain,
With terrors and with clamours compassed round
Of mine own brood, that on my bowels feed:
Thou art my Father, thou my Author, thou
My being gavest me; whom should I obey   865
But thee, whom follow? thou wilt bring me soon
To that new world of light and bliss, among
The Gods who live at ease, where I shall Reign
At thy right hand voluptuous, as beseems
Thy daughter and thy darling, without end'.   870
   Thus saying, from her side the fatal Key,

Sad instrument of all our woe, she took;
And towards the Gate rolling her bestial train,
Forthwith the huge Portcullis high up drew,
Which but her self, not all the *Stygian* powers   875
Could once have moved; then in the key-hole turns
Th' intricate wards, and every Bolt and Bar
Of massy Iron or solid rock with ease
Unfastens: on a sudden open fly
With impetuous recoil and jarring sound   880
Th' infernal doors, and on their hinges grate
Harsh Thunder, that the lowest bottom shook
Of *Erebus*. She opened, but to shut
Excelled her power; the Gates wide open stood,
That with extended wings a Bannered Host   885
Under spread Ensigns marching might pass through
With Horse and Chariots ranked in loose array;
So wide they stood, and like a Furnace mouth
Cast forth redounding smoke and ruddy flame.
Before their eyes in sudden view appear   890
The secrets of the hoary deep, a dark
Illimitable Ocean without bound,
Without dimension; where length, breadth, & height,
And time and place are lost; where eldest *Night*
And *Chaos*, ancestors of Nature, hold   895
Eternal *Anarchy*, amidst the noise
Of endless Wars, and by confusion stand.
For hot, cold, moist, and dry, four Champions fierce
Strive here for Mastry, and to Battle bring
Their embryon Atoms; they around the flag   900
Of each his Faction, in their several Clans,
Light-armed or heavy, sharp, smooth, swift, or slow,
Swarm populous, unnumbered as the Sands
Of *Barca* or *Cyrene's* torrid soil,
Levied to side with warring Winds, and poise   905
Their lighter wings. To whom these most adhere,
He rules a moment; *Chaos* umpire sits,
And by decision more embroils the fray
By which he Reigns: next him high Arbiter
Chance governs all. Into this wild Abyss,   910
The Womb of nature and perhaps her Grave,
Of neither Sea, nor Shore, nor Air, nor Fire,
But all these in their pregnant causes mixed
Confusedly, and which thus must ever fight,
Unless th' Almighty Maker them ordain   915
His dark materials to create more worlds,
Into this wild Abyss the wary fiend
Stood on the brink of Hell and looked a while,
Pondering his Voyage; for no narrow frith

He had to cross. Nor was his ear less pealed   920
With noises loud and ruinous (to compare
Great things with small) than when *Bellona* storms,
With all her battering Engines bent to raze
Some Capital City; or less than if this frame
Of Heav'n were falling, and these Elements   925
In mutiny had from her Axle torn
The steadfast Earth. At last his Sail-broad vans
He spreads for flight, and in the surging smoke
Uplifted spurns the ground, thence many a League
As in a cloudy Chair ascending rides   930
Audacious, but that seat soon failing, meets
A vast vacuity: all unawares
Fluttring his pennons vain plumb down he drops
Ten thousand fadom deep, and to this hour
Down had been falling, had not by ill chance   935
The strong rebuff of some tumultuous cloud
Instinct with Fire and Nitre, hurried him
As many miles aloft: that fury stayed,
Quenched in a boggy *Syrtis*, neither Sea,
Nor good dry Land: nigh foundered on he fares,   940
Treading the crude consistence, half on foot,
Half flying; behoves him now both Oar and Sail.
As when a Gryphon through the Wilderness
With winged course o'er Hill or moory Dale,
Pursues the *Arimaspian*, who by stealth   945
Had from his wakeful custody purloined
The guarded Gold: So eagerly the Fiend
O'er bog or steep, through strait, rough, dense, or rare,
With head, hands, wings or feet pursues his way,
And swims, or sinks, or wades, or creeps, or flies: 950
At length a universal hubbub wild
Of stunning sounds, and voices all confused
Borne through the hollow dark assaults his ear
With loudest vehemence: thither he plies,
Undaunted to meet there what ever power   955
Or Spirit of the nethermost Abyss
Might in that noise reside, of whom to ask
Which way the nearest coast of darkness lies
Bordering on light; when straight behold the Throne
Of *Chaos*, and his dark Pavilion spread   960
Wide on the wasteful Deep; with him enthroned
Sat Sable-vested *Night*, eldest of things,
The consort of his reign; and by them stood
Orcus and *Ades*, and the dreaded name
Of *Demogorgon*; *Rumour* next, and *Chance*,   965
And *Tumult* and *Confusion* all embroiled,
And *Discord* with a thousand various mouths.

    T' whom *Satan*, turning boldly, thus. 'Ye Powers
And Spirits of this nethermost Abyss,
Chaos and *ancient Night*, I come no Spy,   970
With purpose to explore or to disturb
The secrets of your Realm, but by constraint
Wandring this darksome Desert, as my way,
Lies through your spacious Empire up to light,
Alone, and without guide, half lost, I seek   975
What readiest path leads where your gloomy bounds
Confine with Heav'n; or if some other place
From your Dominion won, th' Ethereal King
Possesses lately, thither to arrive
I travel this profound, direct my course;   980
Directed no mean recompense it brings
To your behoof, if I that Region lost,
All usurpation thence expelled, reduce
To her original darkness and your sway
(Which is my present journey) and once more   985
Erect the Standard there of *ancient Night*;
Yours be th' advantage all, mine the revenge'.
    Thus *Satan*; and him thus the Anarch old
With faltring speech and visage incomposed
Answered. 'I know thee, stranger, who thou art,   990
That mighty leading Angel, who of late
Made head against Heav'n's King, though overthrown.
I saw and heard, for such a numerous Host
Fled not in silence through the frighted deep
With ruin upon ruin, rout on rout,   995
Confusion worse confounded; and Heav'n Gates
Poured out by millions her victorious Bands
Pursuing. I upon my Frontiers here
Keep residence; if all I can will serve,
That little which is left so to defend,   1000
Encroached on still through our intestine broils
Weakning the Sceptre of old *Night*: first Hell
Your dungeon, stretching far and wide beneath;
Now lately Heav'n and Earth, another World
Hung o'er my Realm, linked in a golden Chain   1005
To that side Heav'n from whence your Legions fell:
If that way be your walk, you have not far;
So much the nearer danger; go and speed;
Havoc and spoil and ruin are my gain'.
    He ceased; and *Satan* stayed not to reply,   1010
But glad that now his Sea should find a shore,
With fresh alacrity and force renewed
Springs upward like a Pyramid of fire
Into the wild expanse, and through the shock
Of fighting Elements, on all sides round   1015

Environed wins his way; harder beset
And more endangered, than when *Argo* passed
Through *Bosporus* betwixt the justling Rocks:
Or when *Ulysses* on the Larboard shunned
Charybdis, and by th' other whirlpool steered.   1020
So he with difficulty and labour hard
Moved on, with difficulty and labour he;
But he once past, soon after when man fell,
Strange alteration! Sin and Death amain
Following his track, such was the will of Heav'n,   1025
Paved after him a broad and beaten way
Over the dark Abyss, whose boiling Gulf
Tamely endured a Bridge of wondrous length
From Hell continued reaching th' utmost Orb
Of this frail World; by which the Spirits perverse   1030
With easy intercourse pass to and fro
To tempt or punish mortals, except whom
God and good Angels guard by special grace.
   But now at last the sacred influence
Of light appears, and from the walls of Heav'n   1035
Shoots far into the bosom of dim Night
A glimmering dawn; here Nature first begins
Her farthest verge, and *Chaos* to retire
As from her outmost works a broken foe
With tumult less and with less hostile din;   1040
That *Satan* with less toil, and now with ease,
Wafts on the calmer wave by dubious light
And like a weather-beaten Vessel holds
Gladly the Port, though Shrouds and Tackle torn;
Or in the emptier waste, resembling Air,   1045
Weighs his spread wings, at leisure to behold
Far off th' Empyreal Heav'n, extended wide
In circuit, undetermined square or round,
With Opal Towers and Battlements adorned
Of living Sapphire, once his native Seat: 1050
And fast by hanging in a golden Chain
This pendant world, in bigness as a Star
Of smallest Magnitude close by the Moon.
Thither full fraught with mischievous revenge,
Accursed, and in a cursèd hour he hies.   1055

John Dryden
(1631–1700)

Absalom and Achitophel: A Poem

In pious times, ere Priest-craft did begin,
Before *Polygamy* was made a sin;
When man, on many, multiplied his kind,
Ere one to one was, cursedly, confined:
When Nature prompted, and no law denied   5
Promiscuous use of Concubine and Bride;
Then, *Israel*'s Monarch, after Heav'n's own heart,
His vigorous warmth did, variously, impart
To Wives and Slaves: And, wide as his Command,
Scattered his Maker's Image through the Land.   10
Michal, of Royal blood, the Crown did wear,
A Soil ungrateful to the Tiller's care:
Not so the rest; for several Mothers bore
To Godlike *David*, several Sons before.
But since like slaves his bed they did ascend,   15
No True Succession could their seed attend.
Of all this Numerous Progeny was none
So Beautiful so brave as *Absalom*:
Whether, inspired with some diviner Lust,
His Father got him with a greater Gust;   20
Or that his Conscious destiny made way
By manly beauty to Imperial sway.
Early in Foreign fields he won Renown,
With Kings and States allied to *Israel*'s Crown:
In Peace the thoughts of War he could remove,   25
And seemed as he were only born for love.
What e'er he did was done with so much ease,
In him alone, 'twas Natural to please.
His motions all accompanied with grace;
And *Paradise* was opened in his face.   30
With secret Joy, indulgent *David* viewed
His Youthful Image in his Son renewed:
To all his wishes Nothing he denied,
And made the Charming *Annabel* his Bride.
What faults he had (for who from faults is free?)   35
His Father could not, or he would not see.

Some warm excesses, which the Law forbore,
Were construed Youth that purged by boiling o'er:
And *Amnon*'s Murther, by a specious Name,
Was called a Just Revenge for injured Fame.   40
Thus Praised, and Loved, the Noble Youth remained,
While *David*, undisturbed, in *Sion* reigned.
But Life can never be sincerely blest:
Heaven punishes the bad, and proves the best.
The *Jews*, a Headstrong, Moody, Murmuring race,   45
As ever tried th' extent and stretch of grace;
God's pampered people whom, debauched with ease,
No King could govern, nor no God could please;
(Gods they had tried of every shape and size
That God-smiths could produce, or Priests devise.)   50
These *Adam*-wits, too fortunately free,
Began to dream they wanted liberty;
And when no rule, no precedent was found
Of men, by Laws less circumscribed and bound,
They led their wild desires to Woods and Caves,   55
And thought that all but Savages were Slaves.
They who when *Saul* was dead, without a blow,
Made foolish *Isbosheth* the Crown forgo;
Who banished *David* did from *Hebron* bring,
And, with a General Shout, proclaimed him King: 60
Those very *Jews*, who, at their very best,
Their Humour more than Loyalty expressed,
Now, wondered why, so long, they had obeyed
An Idol Monarch which their hands had made.
Thought they might ruin him they could create;   65
Or melt him to that Golden Calf, a State.
But these were random bolts: No formed Design,
Nor Interest made the Factious Crowd to join:
The sober part of *Israel*, free from stain,
Well knew the value of a peaceful reign: 70
And, looking backward with a wise afright,
Saw Seams of wounds, dishonest to the sight;
In contemplation of whose ugly Scars,
They Curst the memory of Civil Wars.
The moderate sort of Men, thus qualified,   75
Inclined the Balance to the better side:
And *David*'s mildness managed it so well,
The Bad found no occasion to Rebel.
But, when to Sin our biased Nature leans,
The careful Devil is still at hand with means;   80
And providently Pimps for ill desires:
The Good old Cause revived, a Plot requires.
Plots, true or false, are necessary things,
To raise up Commonwealths, and ruin Kings.

Th' inhabitants of old *Jerusalem*   85
Were *Jebusites*: the Town so called from them;
And theirs the Native right –
But when the chosen people grew more strong,
The rightful cause at length became the wrong:
And every loss the men of *Jebus* bore,   90
They still were thought God's enemies the more.
Thus, worn and weakened, well or ill content,
Submit they must to *David*'s Government:
Impoverished, and deprived of all Command,
Their Taxes doubled as they lost their Land,   95
And, what was harder yet to flesh and blood,
Their Gods disgraced, and burnt like common wood.
This set the Heathen Priesthood on a flame;
For Priests of all Religions are the same:
Of whatsoe'r descent their Godhead be,   100
Stock, Stone, or other homely pedigree,
In his defense his Servants are as bold
As if he had been born of beaten gold.
The *Jewish Rabbins* though their Enemies,
In this conclude them honest men and wise: 105
For 'twas their duty, all the Learned think,
T' espouse his Cause by whom they eat and drink.
From hence began that Plot, the Nation's Curse,
Bad in itself, but represented worse.
Raised in extremes, and in extremes decried;   110
With Oaths affirmed, with dying Vows denied.
Not weighed, or winnowed by the Multitude;
But swallowed in the Mass, unchewed and Crude.
Some Truth there was, but dashed and brewed with Lies;
To please the Fools, and puzzle all the Wise.   115
Succeeding times did equal folly call,
Believing nothing, or believing all,
Th' *Egyptian* Rites the *Jebusites* embraced;
Where Gods were recommended by their Taste.
Such savory Deities must needs be good,   120
And served at once for Worship and for Food.
By force they could not Introduce these Gods;
For Ten to One, in former days was odds.
So Fraud was used (the Sacrificers' trade),
Fools are more hard to Conquer than Persuade.   125
Their busy Teachers mingled with the *Jews*,
And raked, for Converts, even the Courts and Stews:
Which *Hebrew* Priests the more unkindly took,
Because the Fleece accompanies the Flock.
Some thought they God's Anointed meant to Slay   130
By Guns, invented since full many a day:
Our Author swears it not; but who can know

How far the Devil and *Jebusites* may go?
This Plot, which failed for want of common Sense,
Had yet a deep and dangerous Consequence: 135
For, as when raging Fevers boil the Blood,
The standing Lake soon floats into a Flood;
And every hostile Humour, which before
Slept quiet in its Channels, bubbles o'er:
So, several Factions from this first Ferment,   140
Work up to Foam, and threat the Government.
Some by their Friends, more by themselves thought wise,
Opposed the Power, to which they could not rise.
Some had in Courts been Great, and thrown from thence,
Like Fiends, were hardened in Impenitence.   145
Some by their Monarch's fatal mercy grown,
From Pardoned Rebels, Kinsmen to the Throne;
Were raised in Power and public Office high:
Strong Bands, if Bands ungrateful men could tie.
Of these the false *Achitophel* was first: 150
A Name to all succeeding Ages Cursed.
For close Designs, and crooked Counsel fit;
Sagacious, Bold, and Turbulent of wit:
Restless, unfixed in Principle and Place;
In Power unpleased, impatient of Disgrace.   155
A fiery Soul, which working out its way,
Fretted the Pigmy Body to decay:
And o'er informed the Tenement of Clay.
A daring Pilot in extremity;
Pleased with the Danger, when the Waves went high   160
He sought the Storms; but for a Calm unfit,
Would Steer too nigh the Sands, to boast his Wit.
Great Wits are sure to Madness near allied;
And thin Partitions do their Bounds divide:
Else, why should he, with Wealth and Honour blest,   165
Refuse his Age the needful hours of Rest?
Punish a Body which he could not please;
Bankrupt of Life, yet Prodigal of Ease?
And all to leave, what with his Toil he won,
To that unfeathered, two Leg'd thing, a Son: 170
Got, while his Soul did huddled Notions try;
And born a shapeless Lump, like Anarchy.
In Friendship False, Implacable in Hate:
Resolved to Ruin or to Rule the State.
To Compass this the Triple Bond he broke;   175
The Pillars of the public Safety shook:
And fitted *Israel* for a Foreign Yoke.
Then, seized with Fear, yet still affecting Fame,
Assumed a Patriot's All-atoning Name.
So easy still it proves in Factious Times,   180

With public Zeal to cancel private Crimes:
How safe is Treason, and how sacred ill,
Where none can sin against the People's Will:
Where Crowds can wink; and no offence be known,
Since in another's guilt they find their own.   185
Yet, Fame deserved, no Enemy can grudge;
The Statesman we abhor, but praise the Judge.
In *Israel*'s Courts ne'er sat an *Abbethdin*
With more discerning Eyes, or Hands more clean:
Unbribed, unsought, the Wretched to redress;   190
Swift of Dispatch, and easy of Access.
Oh, had he been content to serve the Crown,
With virtues only proper to the Gown;
Or, had the rankness of the Soil been freed
From Cockle, that oppressed the Noble seed: 195
David, for him his tuneful Harp had strung,
And Heaven had wanted one Immortal song.
But wild Ambition loves to slide, not stand;
And Fortune's Ice prefers to Virtue's Land:
Achitophel, grown weary to possess   200
A lawful Fame, and lazy Happiness;
Disdained the Golden fruit to gather free,
And lent the Crowd his Arm to shake the Tree.
Now, manifest of Crimes, contrived long since,
He stood at bold Defiance with his Prince: 205
Held up the Buckler of the People's Cause,
Against the Crown; and skulked behind the Laws.
The wished occasion of the Plot he takes,
Some Circumstances finds, but more he makes.
By buzzing Emissaries, fills the ears   210
Of list'ning Crowds, with Jealousies and Fears
Of Arbitrary Counsels brought to light,
And proves the King himself a *Jebusite*:
Weak Arguments! which yet he knew full well,
Were strong with People easy to Rebel.   215
For, governed by the *Moon*, the giddy *Jews*
Tread the same track when she the Prime renews:
And once in twenty Years, their Scribes Record,
By natural Instinct they change their, Lord.
Achitophel still wants a Chief, and none   220
Was found so fit as Warlike *Absalom*:
Not, that he wished his Greatness to create,
(For Politicians neither love nor hate):
But, for he knew, his Title not allowed,
Would keep him still depending on the Crowd: 225
That Kingly power, thus ebbing out, might be
Drawn to the dregs of a Democracy.
Him he attempts, with studied Arts to please,

And sheds his Venom, in such words as these.
   'Auspicious Prince! at whose Nativity   230
Some Royal Planet ruled the Southern sky;
Thy longing Country's Darling and Desire;
Their cloudy Pillar, and their guardian Fire:
Their second *Moses*, whose extended Wand
Shuts up the Seas, and shows the promised Land: 235
Whose dawning Day, in every distant age,
Has exercised the Sacred Prophet's rage:
The People's Prayer, the glad Diviner's Theme,
The Young men's Vision, and the Old men's Dream!
Thee, *Saviour*, Thee, the Nation's Vows confess;   240
And, never satisfied with seeing, bless:
Swift, unbespoken Pomps, thy steps proclaim,
And stammering Babes are taught to lisp thy Name.
How long wilt thou the general Joy detain;
Starve, and defraud the People of thy Reign?   245
Content ingloriously to pass thy days
Like one of Virtue's Fools that feed on Praise;
Till thy fresh Glories, which now shine so bright,
Grow Stale and Tarnish with our daily sight.
Believe me, Royal Youth, thy Fruit must be,   250
Or gathered Ripe, or rot upon the Tree.
Heav'n has to all alotted, soon or late,
Some lucky Revolution of their Fate:
Whose Motions, if we watch and guide with Skill
(For human Good depends on human Will),   255
Our Fortune rolls, as from a smooth Descent,
And, from the first Impression, takes the Bent:
But, if unseized, she glides away like wind;
And leaves repenting Folly far behind.
Now, now she meets you, with a glorious prize,   260
And spreads her Locks before her as she flies.
Had thus Old *David*, from whose Loins you spring
Not dared, when Fortune called him, to be King,
At *Gath* an Exile he might still remain,
And heaven's Anointing Oil had been in vain.   265
Let his successful Youth your hopes engage,
But shun th'example of Declining Age:
Behold him setting in his Western Skies,
The Shadows lengthening as the Vapours rise.
He is not now, as when on *Jordan*'s Sand   270
The Joyful People thronged to see him Land,
Cov'ring the *Beach*, and black'ning all the *Strand*:
But, like the Prince of Angels from his height,
Comes tumbling downward with diminished light;
Betrayed by one poor Plot to public Scorn,   275
(Our only blessing since his Cursed Return):

Those heaps of People which one Sheaf did bind,
Blown off and scattered by a puff of Wind.
What strength can he to your Designs oppose,
Naked of Friends, and round beset with Foes?   280
If *Pharoah*'s doubtful Succor he should use,
A Foreign Aid would more Incense the *Jews*:
Proud *Egypt* would dissembled Friendship bring;
Foment the War, but not support the King:
Nor would the Royal Party e'er unite   285
With *Pharoah*'s Arms, t' assist the *Jebusite*;
Or if they should, their Interest soon would break,
And with such odious Aid make *David* weak.
All sorts of men by my successful Arts,
Abhorring Kings, estrange their altered Hearts   290
From *David*'s Rule: And 'tis the general Cry,
Religion, Commonwealth, and Liberty.
If you as Champion of the public Good,
Add to their Arms a Chief of Royal Blood;
What may not *Israel* hope, and what Applause   295
Might such a General gain by such a Cause?
Not barren Praise alone, that Gaudy Flower,
Fair only to the sight, but solid Power:
And Nobler is a limited Command,
Giv'n by the Love of all your Native Land,   300
Than a Successive Title, Long, and Dark,
Drawn from the Mouldy Rolls of *Noah*'s Ark'.
    What cannot Praise effect in Mighty Minds,
When Flattery Soothes, and when Ambition Blinds!
Desire of Power, on Earth a Vicious Weed,   305
Yet, sprung from High, is of Celestial Seed:
In God 'tis Glory: And when men Aspire,
'Tis but a Spark too much of Heavenly Fire.
Th' Ambitious Youth, too Covetous of Fame,
Too full of Angel's Metal in his Frame;   310
Unwarily was led from Virtue's ways;
Made Drunk with Honour, and Debauched with Praise.
Half loath, and half consenting to the Ill,
(For Loyal Blood within him struggled still)
He thus replied – 'And what Pretence have I   315
To take up Arms for Public Liberty?
My Father Governs with unquestioned Right;
The Faith's Defender, and Mankind's Delight:
Good, Gracious, Just, observant of the Laws;
And Heav'n by Wonders has Espoused his Cause.   320
Whom has he Wronged in all his Peaceful Reign?
Who sues for Justice to his Throne in Vain?
What Millions has he Pardoned of his Foes,
Whom Just Revenge did to his Wrath expose?

Mild, Easy, Humble, Studious of our Good;   325
Inclined to Mercy, and averse from Blood.
If Mildness Ill with Stubborn *Israel* Suite,
His Crime is God's beloved Attribute.
What could he gain, his People to Betray,
Or change his Right, for Arbitrary Sway?   330
Let Haughty *Pharoah* Curse with such a Reign,
His Fruitful *Nile*, and Yoke a Servile Train.
If *David*'s Rule *Jerusalem* Displease,
The *Dog-star* heats their Brains to this Disease.
Why then should I, Encouraging the Bad,   335
Turn Rebel, and run Popularly Mad?
Were he a Tyrant who, by Lawless Might,
Oppresed the *Jews*, and Raised the *Jebusite*,
Well might I Mourn; but Nature's Holy Bands
Would Curb my Spirits, and Restrain my Hands: 340
The People might assert their Liberty;
But what was Right in them, were Crime in me.
His Favour leaves me nothing to require;
Prevents my Wishes, and outruns Desire.
What more can I expect while *David* lives,   345
All but his Kingly Diadem he gives:
And that': But there he Paused; then Sighing, said,
'Is Justly Destined for a Worthier Head.
For when my Father from his Toils shall Rest,
And late Augment the Number of the Blest: 350
His Lawful Issue shall the Throne ascend,
Of the *Collateral* Line where that shall end.
His Brother, though Oppressed with Vulgar Spite,
Yet Dauntless and Secure of Native Right,
Of every Royal Virtue stands possessed;   355
Still Dear to all the Bravest, and the Best.
His Courage Foes, his Friends his Truth Proclaim;
His Loyalty the King, the World his Fame.
His Mercy even th' Offending Crowd will find,
For sure he comes of a Forgiving Kind.   360
Why should I then Repine at Heaven's Decree;
Which gives me no Pretence to Royalty?
Yet oh that Fate Propitiously Inclined,
Had raised my Birth, or had debased my Mind;
To my large Soul, not all her Treasure lent,   365
And then Betrayed it to a mean Descent.
I find, I find my mounting Spirits Bold,
And *David*'s Part disdains my Mother's Mold.
Why am I Scanted by a Niggard Birth,
My Soul Disclaims the Kindred of her Earth: 370
And made for Empire, Whispers me within;
Desire of Greatness is a Godlike Sin'.

Him Staggering so when Hell's dire Agent found,
While fainting Virtue scarce maintained her Ground,
He pours fresh Forces in, and thus Replies: 375
    'Th' Eternal God Supremely Good and Wise,
Imparts not these Prodigious Gifts in vain;
What Wonders are Reserved to bless your Reign?
Against your will your Arguments have shown,
Such Virtue's only given to guide a Throne.   380
Not that your Father's mildness I condemn;
But Manly Force becomes the Diadem.
'Tis true, he grants the People all they crave;
And more perhaps than Subjects ought to have:
For Lavish grants suppose a Monarch tame,   385
And more his Goodness than his Wit proclaim.
But when should People strive their Bonds to break,
If not when Kings are Negligent or Weak?
Let him give on till he can give no more,
The Thrifty Sanhedrin shall keep him poor: 390
And every Sheckle which he can receive,
Shall cost a Limb of his Prerogative.
To ply him with new Plots, shall be my care,
Or plunge him deep in some Expensive War;
Which when his Treasure can no more Supply,   395
He must, with the Remains of Kingship, buy.
His faithful Friends, our Jealousies and Fears,
Call *Jebusites*, and *Pharoah*'s Pensioners:
Whom, when our Fury from his Aid has torn,
He shall be Naked left to public Scorn.   400
The next Successor, whom I fear and hate,
My Arts have made Obnoxious to the State;
Turned all his Virtues to his Overthrow,
And gained our Elders to pronounce a Foe.
His Right, for Sums of necessary Gold,   405
Shall first be Pawned, and afterwards be Sold:
Till time shall Ever-wanting *David* draw,
To pass your doubtful Title into Law:
If not; the People have a Right Supreme
To make their Kings; for Kings are made for them.   410
All Empire is no more than Power in Trust,
Which when resumed, can be no longer Just.
Succession, for the general Good designed,
In its own wrong a Nation cannot bind:
If altering that, the People can relieve,   415
Better one Suffer, than a Million grieve.
The *Jews* well know their power: ere *Saul* they Chose,
God was their King, and God they durst Depose.
Urge now your Piety, your Filial Name,
A Father's Right, and fear of Future Fame;   420

The public Good, that Universal Call,
To which even Heav'n Submitted, and answers all.
Nor let his Love Enchant your generous Mind;
'Tis Nature's trick to Propagate her Kind.
Our fond Begetters, who would never die,   425
Love but themselves in their Posterity.
Or let his Kindness by th' Effects be tried,
Or let him lay his vain Pretence aside.
God said he loved your Father; could he bring
A better Proof, than to Anoint him King?   430
It surely showed he loved the Shepherd well,
Who gave so fair a Flock as *Israel*.
Would *David* have you thought his Darling Son?
What means he then, to Alienate the Crown?
The name of Godly he may blush to bear: 435
'Tis after God's own heart to Cheat his Heir.
He to his Brother gives Supreme Command;
To you a Legacy of Barren Land:
Perhaps th' old Harp, on which he thrums his Lays:
Or some dull *Hebrew* Ballad in your Praise.   440
Then the next Heir, a Prince, Severe and Wise,
Already looks on you with Jealous Eyes;
Sees through the thin Disguises of your Arts,
And marks your Progress in the People's Hearts.
Though now his mighty Soul its Grief contains;   445
He meditates Revenge who least Complains.
And like a Lion, Slumbering in the way,
Or Sleep-dissembling, while he waits his Prey,
His fearless Foes within his Distance draws;
Constrains his Roaring, and Contracts his Paws;   450
Till at the last, his time for Fury found,
He shoots with suddain Vengeance from the Ground:
The Prostrate Vulgar, passes o'er, and Spares;
But with a Lordly Rage, his Hunters tears.
Your Case no tame Expedients will afford;   455
Resolve on Death, or Conquest by the Sword,
Which for no less a Stake than Life, you Draw;
And Self-defence is Nature's Eldest Law.
Leave the warm People no Considering time;
For then Rebellion may be thought a Crime.   460
Prevail yourself of what Occasion gives,
But try your Title while your Father lives:
And that your Arms may have a fair Pretence,
Proclaim, you take them in the King's Defence:
Whose Sacred life each minute would Expose,   465
To Plots, from seeming Friends, and secret Foes.
And who can sound the depth of *David*'s Soul?
Perhaps his fear, his kindness may Control.

He fears his Brother, though he loves his Son,
For plighted Vows too late to be undone. 470
If so, by Force he wishes to be gained,
Like women's Lechery, to seem Constrained:
Doubt not, but when he most affects the Frown,
Commit a pleasing Rape upon the Crown.
Secure his Person to secure your Cause; 475
They who possess the Prince, possess the Laws'.
   He said, And this Advice above the rest,
With *Absalom*'s Mild nature suited best;
Unblamed of Life (Ambition set aside),
Not stained with Cruelty, nor puffed with Pride; 480
How happy had he been, if Destiny
Had higher placed his Birth, or not so high?
His Kingly Virtues might have claimed a Throne,
And blessed all other Countries but his own:
But charming Greatness, since so few refuse; 485
'Tis Juster to Lament him, than Accuse.
Strong were his hopes a Rival to remove,
With blandishments to gain the public Love;
To Head the Faction while their Zeal was hot,
And Popularly prosecute the Plot. 490
To farther this, *Achitophel* Unites
The Malcontents of all the *Israelites*,
Whose differing Parties he could widely Join,
For several Ends, to serve the same Design.
The Best, and of the Princes some were such, 495
Who thought the power of Monarchy too much:
Mistaken Men, and Patriots in their Hearts;
Not Wicked, but Seduced by Impious Arts.
By these the Springs of Property were bent,
And wound so high, they Cracked the Government. 500
The next for Interest sought t' embroil the State,
To sell their Duty at a dearer rate;
And make their *Jewish* Markets of the Throne,
Pretending public Good, to serve their own.
Others thought Kings an useless heavy Load, 505
Who Cost too much, and did too little Good.
These were for laying Honest *David* by,
On Principles of pure good Husbandry.
With them Joined all th' Haranguers of the Throng,
That thought to get Preferment by the Tongue. 510
Who follow next, a double Danger bring,
Not only hating *David*, but the King,
The *Solymaean* Rout; well Versed of old,
In Godly Faction, and in Treason bold;
Cowering and Quaking at a Conqueror's Sword, 515
But Lofty to a Lawful Prince Restored;

Saw with Disdain an *Ethnic* Plot begun,
And Scorned by *Jebusites* to be Outdone.
Hot *Levites* Headed these; who pulled before
From th' *Ark*, which in the Judges days they bore,   520
Resumed their Cant, and with a Zealous Cry,
Pursued their old beloved Theocracy;
Where Sanhedrin and Priest enslaved the Nation,
And justified their Spoils by Inspiration;
For who so fit for Reign as *Aaron*'s Race,   525
If once Dominion they could found in Grace?
These led the Pack; though not of surest scent,
Yet deepest mouthed against the Government.
A numerous Host of dreaming Saints succeed;
Of the true old Enthusiastic breed: 530
'Gainst Form and Order they their Power employ;
Nothing to Build and all things to Destroy.
But far more numerous was the herd of such,
Who think too little, and talk too much.
These, out of mere instinct, they knew not why,   535
Adored their fathers' God, and Property:
And, by the same blind benefit of Fate,
The Devil and the Jebusite did hate:
Born to be saved, even in their own despight;
Because they could not help believing right.   540
Such were the tools; but a whole Hydra more
Remains, of sprouting heads too long, to score.
Some of their Chiefs were Princes of the Land:
In the first Rank of these did *Zimri* stand:
A man so various, that he seemed to be   545
Not one, but all Mankind's Epitome.
Stiff in Opinions, always in the wrong;
Was everything by starts, and nothing long:
But, in the course of one revolving Moon,
Was Chemist, Fiddler, Statesman, and Buffoon   550
Then all for Women, Painting, Rhyming, Drink
Besides ten thousand freaks that died in thinking.
Blessed Madman, who could every hour employ,
With something new to wish, or to enjoy!
Railing and praising were his usual Themes;   555
And both (to show his Judgement) in Extremes:
So over-Violent, or over-Civil,
That every man, with him, was God or Devil.
In squandering Wealth was his peculiar Art:
Nothing went unrewarded, but Desert.   560
Beggared by Fools, whom still he found too late:
He had his Jest, and they had his Estate.
He laughed himself from Court, then sought Relief
By forming Parties, but could ne'er be Chief:

For, spite of him, the weight of Business fell   565
On *Absalom* and wise *Achitophel*:
Thus, wicked but in will, of means bereft,
He left not Faction, but of that was left.
   Titles and Names 'twere tedious to Rehearse
Of Lords, below the Dignity of Verse.   570
Wits, warriors, Commonwealths-men, were the best:
Kind Husbands and mere Nobles all the rest.
And, therefore in the name of Dulness, be
The well-hung *Balaam* and cold *Caleb* free.
And Canting *Nadab* left Oblivion damn,   575
Who made new porridge for the Paschal Lamb.
Let Friendship's holy band some Names assure:
Some their own Worth, and some let Scorn secure.
Nor shall the Rascal Rabble here have Place,
Whom Kings no Titles gave, and God no Grace: 580
Not Bull-faced *Jonas*, who could Statutes draw
To mean Rebellion, and make Treason Law.
But he, though bad, is followed by a worse,
The wretch, who Heaven's Annointed dared to Curse.
Shimei, whose early Youth did Promise bring   585
Of Zeal to God, and Hatred to his King;
Did wisely from Expensive Sins refrain,
And never broke the Sabbath, but for Gain:
Nor ever was known an Oath to vent,
Or Curse unless against the Government.   590
Thus, heaping Wealth, by the most ready way
Among the Jews, which was to Cheat and Pray;
The City, to reward his pious Hate
Against his Master, chose him Magistrate:
His Hand a Vare of Justice did uphold;   595
His Neck was loaded with a Chain of Gold.
During his Office, Treason was no Crime.
The Sons of *Belial* had a glorious Time:
For *Shimei*, though not prodigal or pelf,
Yet loved his wicked Neighbour as himself: 600
When two or three were gathered to declaim
Against the Monarch of *Jerusalem*,
Shimei was always in the midst of them.
And, if they Cursed the King when he was by,
Would rather Curse, than break good Company.   605
If any durst his Factious Friends accuse,
He packed a Jury of dissenting Jews:
Whose fellow-feeling, in the godly Cause,
Would free the suff'ring Saint from Human Laws.
For Laws are only made to Punish those,   610
Who serve the King, and to protect his Foes.
If any leisure time he had from Power

(Because 'tis Sin to misimploy an hour),
His business was, by Writing, to Persuade,
That Kings were Useless, and a Clog to Trade: 615
And, that his noble Style he might refine,
No *Rechabite* more shunned the fumes or Wine.
Chaste were his Cellars, and his Shrieval Board
The Grossness of a City Feast abhorred:
His Cooks, with long disuse, their Trade forgot;   620
Cool was his Kitchen, though his Brains were hot.
Such frugal Virtue Malice may accuse,
But sure 'twas necessary to the Jews:
For Towns once burnt, such Magistrates require
As dare not tempt God's Providence by fire.   625
With Spiritual food he fed his Servants well,
But free from flesh, that made the Jews Rebel:
And *Moses*'s Laws he held in more account,
For forty days of Fasting in the Mount.
    To speak the rest, who better are forgot,   630
Would tire a well-breathed Witness of the Plot:
Yet, *Corah*, thou shalt from Oblivion pass;
Erect thy self thou Monumental Brass:
High as the Serpent of thy metal made,
While Nations stand secure beneath thy shade.   635
What though this Bird were base, yet Comets rise
From Earthly Vapours ere they shine in Skies.
Prodigious Actions may as well be done
By Weaver's issue, as by Prince's Son.
This Arch-Attestor for the Public Good,   640
by that one Deed Ennobles all his Blood.
Who ever asked the Witnesses' high race,
Whose Oath with Martyrdom did *Stephen* grace?
Ours was a *Levite*, and as times went then,
His Tribe was God Almighty's Gentlemen.   645
Sunk were his Eyes, his Voice was harsh and loud,
Sure signs he neither Choleric was, nor Proud:
His long Chin proved his Wit; his Saintlike Grace
A Church Vermilion, and a *Moses*'s Face;
His Memory, miraculously great,   650
Could Plots, exceeding man's belief, repeat;
Which, therefore cannot be accounted Lies,
For human Wit could never such devise.
Some future Truths are mingled in his Book;
But, where the witness failed, the Prophet Spoke: 655
Some things like Visionary flights appear;
The Spirit caught him up, the Lord knows where:
And gave him his *Rabinical* degree
Unknown to Foreign University.
His Judgement yet his Memory did excel;   660

Which pieced his wondrous Evidence so well:
And suited to the temper of the times;
Then groaning under Jebusitic Crimes.
Let *Israel*'s foes suspect his heav'nly call,
And rashly judge his wit Apocryphal;   665
Our Laws for such affronts have forfeits made:
He takes his life, who takes away his trade.
Were I myself in witness *Corah's* place,
The wretch who did me such a dire disgrace,
Should whet my memory, though once forgot,   670
To make him an Appendix of my Plot.
His Zeal to Heav'n, made him his Prince despise,
And load his person with indignities:
But Zeal peculiar privilege affords;
Indulging latitude to deeds and words.   675
And *Corah* might for *Agag's* murder call,
In terms as coarse as *Samuel* used to *Saul.*
What others in his Evidence did Join,
(The best that could be had for love of coin),
In *Corah's* own predicament will fall: 680
For *witness* is a Common Name to all.
   Surrounded thus with Friends of every sort,
Deluded *Absalom*, forsakes the Court:
Impatient of high hopes, urged with renown,
And Fired with near possession of a Crown,   685
Th' admiring Crowd are dazzled with surprise,
And on his goodly person feed their eyes:
Dissembling Joy, he sets himself to show;
On each side bowing popularly low:
His looks, his gestures, and his words he frames,   690
And with familiar ease repeats their Names.
Thus, formed by Nature, furnished out with Arts,
He glides unfelt into their secret hearts:
Then with a kind compassionate look,
And sighs, bespeaking pity ere he spoke,   695
Few words he said; but easy those and fit:
More slow than Hybla drops, and far more sweet.
   'I mourn, my Countrymen, your lost Estates;
Though far unable to prevent your fate:
Behold a Banished man, for your dear cause   700
Exposed a prey to Arbitrary laws!
Yet oh! that I alone could be undone,
Cut off from Empire, and no more a Son!
Now all your Liberties a spoil are made;
Egypt and *Tyrus* intercept your Trade,   705
And Jebusites your Sacred Rites invade.
My Father, whom with reverence yet I name,
Charmed into Ease, is careless of his Fame:

And, bribed with petty sums of Foreign Gold,
Is grown in *Bathsheba*'s Embraces old: 710
Exalts his Enemies, his Friends destroys:
And all his power against himself employs.
He gives, and let him give my right away:
But why should he his own, and yours betray?
He only, he can make the Nation bleed,   715
And he alone from my revenge is freed.
Take then my tears (with that he wiped his Eyes)
'Tis all the Aid my present power supplies:
No Court Informer can these Arms accuse,
These Arms may Sons against their Fathers use,   720
And, 'tis my wish, the next Successor's Reign
May make no other Israelite complain'.
   Youth, Beauty, Graceful Action, seldom fail:
But Common Interest always will prevail:
And pity never Ceases to be shown   725
To him, who makes the people's wrongs his own.
The Crowd (that still believes their Kings oppress)
With lifted hands their young *Messiah* bless:
Who now begins his Progress to ordain;
With Chariots, Horsemen, and a numerous train: 730
From East to West his Glories he displays:
And, like the Sun, the promised land surveys.
Fame runs before him, as the morning Star;
And shouts of Joy salute him from afar:
Each house receives him as a Guardian God;   735
And Consecrates the Place of his abode:
But hospitable treats did most Commend
Wise *Issachar*, his wealthy western friend.
This moving Court, that caught the people's Eyes
And seemed but Pomp, did other ends disguise: 740
Achitophel had formed it, with intent
To sound the depth, and fathom where it went:
The People's hearts, distinguish Friends from Foes;
And try their strength, before they came to blows:
Yet all was coloured with a smooth pretence   745
Of specious love, and duty to their Prince.
Religion, and Redress of Grievances,
Two names, that always cheat and always please,
Are often urged; and good King *David*'s life
Endangered by a Brother and a Wife.   750
Thus, in a Pageant Show, a Plot is made;
And Peace itself is War in Masquerade.
Oh foolish *Israel*! never warned by ill,
Still the same bait, and circumvented still!
Did ever men forsake their present ease,   755
In midst of health Imagine a disease;

Take pains Contingent mischiefs to foresee,
Make Heirs for Monarchs, and for God decree?
What shall we think! can People give away
Both for themselves and Sons, their Native sway?   760
Then they are left Defenseless, to the Sword
Of each unbounded Arbitrary Lord:
And Laws are vain, by which we Right enjoy,
If Kings unquestioned can those laws destroy.
Yet, if the Crowd be Judge of fit and Just,   765
And Kings are only Officers in trust,
Then this resuming Cov'nant was declared
When Kings were made, or is for ever barred:
If those who gave the Sceptre, could not tie
By their own deed their own Posterity,   770
How then could *Adam* bind his future Race?
How could his forfeit on mankind take place?
Or how could heavenly Justice damn us all,
Who ne'er consented to our Father's fall?
Then Kings are slaves to those whom they Command,   775
And Tenants to their People's pleasure stand.
That Power, which is for Property allowed,
Is mischievously seated in the Crowd:
For who can be secure of private Right,
If Sovereign sway may be dissolved by might?   780
Nor is the People's Judgement always true:
The most may err as grossly as the few,
And faultless Kings run down, by Common Cry,
For Vice, Oppression, and for Tyranny.
What Standard is there in a fickle rout,   785
Which flowing to the mark, runs faster out?
Nor only Crowds, but Sanhedrins may be
Infected with this public Lunacy:
And Share the madness of Rebellious times,
To Murder Monarchs for Imagined crimes.   790
If they may Give and Take when e'er they please,
Not Kings alone (the Godhead's Image),
But Government itself at length must fall
To Nature's state; where all have Right to all.
Yet, grant our Lords the People Kings can make,   795
What Prudent men a settled Throne would shake?
For whatso'er their Sufferings were before,
That Change they Covet makes them suffer more.
All other Errors but disturb a State;
But Innovation is the Blow of Fate.   800
If ancient Fabrics nod, and threat to fall,
To Patch the Flaws, and Buttress up the Wall,
Thus far 'tis Duty; but here fix the Mark:
For all beyond is to touch our Ark.

To change Foundations, cast the Frame anew,   805
Is work for Rebels who base Ends pursue:
At once Divine and Human Laws control;
And mend the Parts by ruin of the Whole.
The Tampering World is subject to this Curse,
To Physic their Disease into a worse.   810
   Now what Relief can Righteous *David* bring?
How Fatal 'tis to be too good a King!
Friends he has few, so high the Madness grows;
Who dare be such, must be the People's Foes:
Yet some there were, ev'n in the worst of days;   815
Some let me name, and Naming is to praise.
   In this short File *Barzillai* first appears;
Barzillai crowned with Honour and with Years:
Long since, the rising Rebels he withstood
In Regions Waste, beyond the *Jordan*'s Flood: 820
Unfortunately Brave to buoy the State;
But sinking underneath his Master's Fate:
In Exile with his Godlike Prince he Mourned;
For him he Suffered, and with him Returned.
The Court he practised, not the Courtier's art: 825
Large was his Wealth, but larger was his Heart:
Which, well the Noblest Objects knew to choose,
The Fighting Warrior, and Recording Muse.
His Bed could once a Fruitful Issue boast:
Now more than half a Father's Name is lost.   830
His Eldest Hope, with every Grace adorned,
By me (so Heav'n will have it) always Mourned,
And always honoured, snatched in Manhood's prime
By unequal Fates, and Providence's crime:
Yet not before the Goal of Honour won,   835
All parts fulfilled of Subject and of Son;
Swift was the Race, but short the Time to run.
Oh Narrow Circle, but of Power Divine,
Scanted in Space, but perfect in thy Line!
By Sea, by Land, thy Matchless Worth was known;   840
Arms thy Delight, and War was all thy Own:
Thy force, Infused, the fainting *Tyrians* propped:
And Haughty *Pharaoh* found his Fortune stopped.
Oh Ancient Honour, Oh Unconquered Hand,
Whom Foes unpunished never could withstand!   845
But *Israel* was unworthy of thy Birth;
Short is the date of all Immoderate Worth.
It looks as Heaven our Ruin has designed,
And durst not trust thy Fortune and thy Mind.
Now, free from Earth, thy disencumbered Soul   850
Mounts up, and leaves behind the Clouds and Starry Pole:
From thence thy kindred legions mayst thou bring

To aid the guardian Angel of thy King.
Here stop my Muse, here cease thy painful flight;
No Pinions can pursue Immortal height: 855
Tell good *Barzillai* thou canst sing no more,
And tell thy Soul she should have fled before;
Or fled she with his life, and left this Verse
To hang on her departed Patron's Hearse?
Now take thy steepy flight from heaven, and see   860
If thou canst find on earth another *He*,
Another he would be too hard to find,
See then whom thou canst see not far behind.
Zadock the Priest, whom, shunning Power and Place,
His lowly mind advanced to *David*'s Grace: 865
With him the *Sagan* of *Jerusalem*,
Of hospitable Soul and noble Stem;
Him of the Western dome, whose weighty sense
Flows in fit words and heavenly eloquence.
The Prophets' Sons by such example led,   870
To Learning and to Loyalty were bred:
For *Colleges* on bounteous Kings depend,
And never Rebel was to Arts a friend.
To these succeed the Pillars of the Laws,
Who best could plead and best can judge a Cause.   875
Next them a train of Loyal Peers ascend:
Sharp judging *Adriel* the Muses' friend,
Himself a Muse – In Sanhedrin's debate
True to his Prince; but not a Slave of State,
Whom *David*'s love with Honours did adorn,   880
That from his disobedient Son were torn.
Jotham of ready wit and pregnant thought,
Endued by nature, and by learning taught
To move Assemblies, who but only tried
The worse awhile, then chose the better side;   885
Nor chose alone, but turned the balance too;
So much the weight of one brave man can do.
Hushai the friend of *David* in distress,
In public storms of manly stedfastness;
By foreign treaties he informed his Youth;   890
And joined experience to his native truth.
His frugal care supplied the wanting Throne,
Frugal for that, but bounteous of his own:
'Tis easy conduct when Exchequers flow,
But hard the task to manage well the low: 895
For Sovereign power is too depressed or high,
When Kings are forced to sell, or Crowds to buy.
Indulge one labour more my weary Muse,
For *Amiel*, who can *Amiel*'s praise refuse?
Of ancient race by birth, but nobler yet   900

In his own worth, and without Title great:
The Sanhedrin long time as chief he ruled,
Their Reason guided and their Passion cooled;
So dexterous was he in the Crown's defence,
So formed to speak a Loyal Nation's Sense,   905
That as their band was *Israel*'s Tribes in small,
So fit was he to represent them all.
Now rather Charioteers the Seat ascend,
Whose loose Careers his steady Skill commend:
They like th' unequal Ruler of the Day,   910
Misguide the Seasons and Mistake the Way;
While he withdrawn at their mad Labour smiles,
And safe enjoys the Sabbath of his Toils.
    These were the chief, a small but faithful Band
Of Worthies, in the Breach who dared to stand,   915
And tempt th' united Fury of the Land.
With grief they viewed such powerful Engines bent,
To batter down the lawful Government.
A numerous Faction with pretended frights,
In Sanhedrins to plume the Regal Rights: 920
The true Successor from the Court removed;
The Plot, by hireling Witnesses improved.
These Ills they saw, and, as their Duty bound,
They showed the King the danger of the Wound:
That no Concessions from the Throne would please,   925
But Lenitives fomented the Disease:
That *Absalom*, ambitious of the Crown,
Was made the Lure to draw the People down:
That false *Achitophel*'s pernicious Hate,
Had turned the Plot to Ruin Church and State: 930
The Council violent, the Rabble worse:
That *Shimei* taught *Jerusalem* to Curse.
    With all these loads of Injuries oppressed,
And long revolving, in his careful Breast,
Th' event of things; at last his patience tired,   935
Thus from his Royal Throne by Heav'n inspired,
The God-like *David* spoke: with awful fear
His Train their Maker in their Master hear.
    'Thus long have I by native mercy swayed,
My wrongs dissembled, my revenge delayed: 940
So willing to forgive th' Offending Age,
So much the Father did the King assuage.
But now so far my Clemency they slight,
Th'Offenders question my Forgiving Right.
That one was made for many, they contend: 945
But 'tis to Rule, for that's a Monarch's End.
They call my tenderness of Blood, my Fear:
Though Manly tempers can the longest bear.

Yet, since they will divert my Native course,
'Tis time to show I am not Good by Force.   950
Those heaped Affronts that haughty Subjects bring,
Are burdens for a Camel, not a King:
Kings are the public Pillars of the State,
Born to sustain and prop the Nation's weight:
If my Young *Samson* will pretend a Call   955
To shake the Column, let him share the Fall:
But oh that yet he would repent and live!
How easy 'tis for Parents to forgive!
With how few Tears a Pardon might be won
From Nature, pleading for a Darling Son!   960
Poor pitied Youth by my Paternal care,
Raised up to all the Height his Frame could bear:
Had God ordained his fate for Empire born,
He would have given his Soul another turn:
Gulled with a Patriot's name, whose Modern sense   965
Is one that would by Law destroy his Prince:
The People's Brave, the Politician's Tool;
Never was Patriot yet, but was a Fool.
Whence comes it that Religion and the Laws
Should more be *Absalom*'s than *David*'s Cause?   970
His old Instructor, ere he lost his Place,
Was never thought endued with so much Grace.
Good Heav'ns, how Faction can a Patriot Paint!
My Rebel ever proves my People's Saint:
Would *They* impose an Heir upon the Throne?   975
Let Sanhedrins be taught to give their Own.
A King's at least a part of Government,
And mine as requisite as their Consent:
Without my Leave a future King to choose,
Infers a Right the Present to Depose: 980
True, they Petition me t' approve their Choice,
But *Esau*'s Hands suit ill with *Jacob*'s Voice.
My Pious Subjects for my Safety pray,
Which to Secure they take my Power away.
From Plots and Treasons Heaven preserve my years,   985
But Save me most from my Petitioners.
Unsatiate as the barren Womb or Grave;
God cannot Grant so much as they can Crave.
What then is left but with a Jealous Eye
To guard the Small remains of Royalty?   990
The Law shall still direct my *peaceful* Sway,
And the same Law teach Rebels to Obey:
Votes shall no more Established Power control,
Such Votes as make a Part exceed the Whole:
No groundless Clamours shall my Friends remove,   995
Nor Crowds have power to Punish ere they Prove:

For Gods, and Godlike Kings their care express,
Still to Defend their Servants in distress.
Oh that my Power to Saving were confined:
Why am I forced, like Heaven, against my mind,   1000
To make Examples of another Kind?
Must I at length the Sword of Justice draw?
Oh cursed Effects of necessary Law!
How ill my Fear they by my Mercy scan,
Beware the Fury of a Patient Man.   1005
Law they require, let Law then show her Face;
They could not be content to look on Grace,
Her hinder parts, but with a daring Eye
To tempt the terror of her Front, and Die.
By their own arts 'tis Righteously decreed,   1010
Those dire Artificers of Death shall bleed.
Against themselves their Witnesses will Swear,
Till Viper-like their Mother Plot they tear:
And suck for nutriment that bloody gore
Which was their Principle of Life before.   1015
Their *Belial* with their *Belzebub* will fight;
Thus on my Foes, my Foes shall do me Right:
Nor doubt th'event: for Factious crowds engage
In their first Onset, all their Brutal Rage;
Then, let 'em take an unresisted Course,   1020
Retire and Traverse, and Delude their Force:
But when they stand all Breathless, urge the fight,
And rise upon 'em with redoubled might:
For Lawful Power is still Superior found,
When long driven back, at length it stands the ground'.   1025
    He said. Th' Almighty, nodding, gave Consent;
And Peals of Thunder shook the Firmament.
Henceforth a Series of new time began,
The mighty Years in long Procession ran:
Once more the Godlike *David* was Restored,   1030
And willing Nations knew their Lawful Lord.

To the Memory of Mr *Oldham*

Farewell, too little and too lately known,
Whom I began to think and call my own;
For sure our Souls were near allied; and thine
Cast in the same Poetic mould with mine.
One common Note on either Lyre did strike,   5
And Knaves and Fools were both abhorred alike:
To the same Goal did both our Studies drive,
The last set out the soonest did arrive.
Thus *Nisus* fell upon the slippery place,

While his young Friend performed and won the Race.   10
O early ripe! to thy abundant store
What could advancing Age have added more?
It might (what Nature never gives the young)
Have taught the numbers of thy native Tongue.
But Satire needs not those, and Wit will shine   15
Through the harsh cadence of a rugged line.
A noble Error, and but seldom made,
When Poets are by too much force betrayed,
Thy generous fruits, though gathered ere their prime
Still showed a quickness; and maturing time   20
But mellows what we write to the dull sweets of Rhyme.
Once more, hail and farewell; farewell thou young
But ah too short, *Marcellus* of our Tongue;
Thy Brows with Ivy, and with Laurels bound;
But Fate and gloomy Night encompass thee around.   25

A Song for St Cecilia's Day

1

From Harmony, from heav'nly Harmony
    This Universal Frame began.
    When Nature underneath a heap
    Of jarring Atoms lay,
    And could not heave her Head,   5
The tuneful Voice was heard from high,
    Arise ye more than dead.
Then cold, and hot, and moist, and dry,
In order to their stations leap,
    And MUSIC's pow'r obey.   10
From Harmony, from Heav'nly Harmony
    This universal Frame began:
    From Harmony to Harmony
Through all the compass of the Notes it ran,
The Diapason closing full in Man.   15

2

What Passion cannot MUSIC raise and quell!
    When Jubal struck the corded Shell,
   His List'ning Brethren stood around
   And wond'ring, on their Faces fell
   To worship that Celestial Sound.   20
Less than a God they thought there could not dwell
    Within the hollow of that Shell
    That spoke so sweetly and so well.
What Passion cannot MUSIC raise and quell!

3

The TRUMPET's loud Clangor   25
   Excites us to Arms
With shrill Notes of Anger
   And mortal Alarms.
The double double double beat
   Of the thundring DRUM   30
Cries, hark the Foes come;
Charge, Charge, 'tis too late to retreat.

4

The soft complaining FLUTE
In dying Notes discovers
   The Woes of hopeless Lovers,   35
Whose Dirge is whispered by the warbling LUTE.

5

Sharp VIOLINS proclaim
Their jealous Pangs, and Desperation,
Fury, frantic Indignation,
Depth of Pains, and height of Passion,   40
   For the fair, disdainful Dame.

6

But oh! what Art can teach
   What human Voice can reach
The sacred Organ's praise?
Notes inspiring holy Love,   45
Notes that wing their heav'nly ways
   To mend the Choirs above.

7

Orpheus could lead the savage race;
And Trees unrooted left their place;
   Sequacious of the Lyre: 50
But bright *CECILIA* raised the wonder higher;
When to her ORGAN, vocal Breath was giv'n
An Angel heard, and straight appeared
   Mistaking Earth for Heaven.

Grand Chorus

As from the pow'r of sacred Lays   55
   The Spheres began to move,
And sung the great Creator's praise
   To all the blessed above;

So when the last and dreadful hour
This crumbling Pageant shall devour,   60
The TRUMPET *shall be heard on high,*
The Dead shall live, the Living die,
And MUSIC *shall untune the Sky.*

John Wilmot, Earl of Rochester (1647–1680)

The Imperfect Enjoyment

Naked she lay, clasped in my longing Arms,
I filled with Love, and she all over Charms;
Both equally inspired with eager fire,
Melting through kindness, flaming in desire.
With *Arms, Legs, Lips* close clinging to embrace,　　　　　5
She clips me to her *Breast*, and sucks me to her *Face*.
Her nimble *Tongue* (*Love*'s lesser Lightning) played
Within my *Mouth*, and to my thoughts conveyed
Swift Orders that I should prepare to throw
The *All-dissolving Thunderbolt* below.　　　　　10
My flutt'ring *Soul*, sprung with the pointed Kiss,
Hangs hov'ring o'er her *Balmy Lips* of Bliss.
But whilst her busy hand would guide that part,
Which should convey my *Soul* up to her *Heart*,
In Liquid *Raptures* I dissolve all o'er,　　　　　15
Melt into Sperm, and spend at every Pore.
A touch from any part of her had done 't:
Her Hand, her Foot, her very Look's a *Cunt*.
　　Smiling, she Chides in a kind murm'ring *Noise*,
And from her Body wipes the Clammy Joys,　　　　　20
When, with a Thousand Kisses wand'ring o'er
My panting Bosom, 'Is there then no more?'
She cries. 'All this to Love and Rapture's due;
Must we not pay a Debt to Pleasure too?'
　　But I, the most forlorn, lost Man alive,　　　　　25
To show my wished Obedience vainly strive:
I Sigh, alas! and Kiss, but cannot *Swive*.
Eager desires confound my first intent,
Succeeding shame does more success prevent,
And Rage at last confirms me Impotent.　　　　　30
Ev'n her fair Hand, which might bid heat return
To frozen Age, and make cold *Hermits* burn,
Applied to my dead *Cinder*, warms no more
Than Fire to Ashes could past Flames restore.
Trembling, confused, despairing, limber, dry,　　　　　35
A wishing, weak, unmoving Lump I lie.

This *Dart* of Love, whose piercing point, oft tried,
With *Virgin blood Ten Thousand Maids* has dyed;
Which *Nature* still directed with such *Art*
That it through every *Cunt* reached every *Heart* –   40
Stiffly resolved, 'twould carelessly invade
Woman or *Boy*, nor aught its fury stayed:
Where e'er it pierced, a *Cunt* it found or made –
Now languid lies in this unhappy hour,
Shrunk up and Sapless like a withered *Flower*.   45
  Thou treacherous, base deserter of my flame,
False to my Passion, fatal to my Fame,
Through what mistaken *Magic* dost thou prove
So true to Lewdness, so untrue to Love?
What *Oyster-Cinder-Beggar*-Common *Whore*   50
Didst thou e'er fail in all thy Life before?
When *Vice, Disease*, and *Scandal* lead the way,
With what officious haste dost thou obey!
Like a Rude, roaring *Hector* in the Streets
Who Scuffles, Cuffs, and Justles all he meets,   55
But if his King or Country claim his Aid,
The *Rascal Villain* shrinks and hides his Head;
Ev'n so thy Brutal Valour is displayed,
Breaks every *Stew*, does each small *Whore invade*,
But if great *Love* the onset does command,   60
Base Recreant to thy *Prince*, thou dar'st not stand.
Worst part of me, and henceforth hated most,
Through all the *Town* a common *Fucking Post*,
On whom each *Whore* relieves her tingling *Cunt*
As *Hogs* on gates do rub themselves and grunt,   65
Mayst thou to rav'nous *Cankers* be a *Prey*,
Or in consuming *Weepings* waste away;
May *Stranguries and Stone* thy *Days* attend;
May'st thou ne'er Piss, who didst refuse to spend
When all my Joys did on False thee depend.   70
  And may *Ten Thousand* abler *Pricks* agree
  To do the wronged *Corinna* right for thee.

A Satyr against Reason and Mankind

  Were I (who to my cost already am
One of those strange, prodigious Creatures, Man)
A Spirit free to choose, for my own share,
What Case of Flesh and Blood I pleased to wear,
I'd be a Dog, a Monkey, or a Bear,   5
Or anything but that vain Animal
Who is so Proud of being Rational.
  The Senses are too gross, and he'll contrive

A Sixth, to contradict the other Five,
And before certain Instinct, will prefer   10
Reason, which fifty times for one does err;
Reason, an *Ignis fatuus* in the Mind,
Which, leaving Light of Nature, Sense, behind,
Pathless and dang'rous wand'ring ways it takes
Through Error's Fenny Bogs and Thorny Brakes;   15
Whilst the misguided Follower climbs with pain
Mountains of Whimsies, heaped in his own Brain;
Stumbling from Thought to Thought, falls headlong down
Into Doubt's boundless Sea, where, like to drown,
Books bear him up awhile, and make him try   20
To swim with Bladders of Philosophy;
In hopes still to o'ertake th' escaping Light,
The Vapour dances in his dazzling sight
Till, spent, it leaves him to eternal Night.
Then Old Age and Experience, hand in hand,   25
Lead him to Death, and make him understand,
After a Search so painful and so long,
That all his Life he has been in the wrong.
Huddled in Dirt the Reasoning Engine lies,
Who was so Proud, so Witty, and so Wise.   30
    Pride drew him in, as Cheats their Bubbles catch,
And made him venture to be made a Wretch.
His Wisdom did his Happiness destroy,
Aiming to know that World he should enjoy.
And Wit his vain, frivolous Pretence   35
Of pleasing others at his own Expense,
For Wits are treated just like Common Whores:
First they're enjoyed, and then kicked out of Doors.
The Pleasure past, a threat'ning Doubt remains
That frights th' Enjoyer with succeeding Pains.   40
Women and Men of Wit are dangerous Tools,
And ever fatal to admiring Fools:
Pleasure allures, and when the *Fops* escape,
'Tis not that they're belov'd, but fortunate,
And therefore what they fear, at last they hate.   45
    But now, methinks, some formal Band and Beard
Takes me to task. Come on, Sir; I'm prepared.
    'Then, by your favour, anything that's writ
Against this gibing, jingling knack called *Wit*
Likes me abundantly, but you take care   50
Upon this point, not to be too severe.
Perhaps my *Muse* were fitter for this part,
For I profess, I can be very smart
On *Wit*, which I abhor with all my Heart.
I long to lash it in some sharp Essay,   55
But your grand indiscretion bids me stay

And turns my Tide of Ink another way.
What rage ferments in your degen'rate Mind
To make you Rail at Reason and Mankind?
Blest, glorious *Man*! to whom alone kind *Heav'n*   60
An everlasting *Soul* has freely giv'n,
Whom his great *Maker* took such care to make
That from himself he did the *Image* take
And this fair frame in shining *Reason* dressed
To dignify his Nature above *Beast*;   65
Reason, by whose aspiring influence
We take a flight beyond material sense,
Dive into Mysteries, then soaring pierce
The flaming limits of the Universe,
Search Heav'n and Hell, find out what's Acted there,   70
And give the World true grounds of hope and fear'.
   'Hold, mighty man', I cry, 'all this we know
From the Pathetic Pen of *Ingelo*,
From *Patrick's Pilgrim, Sibbes'* soliloquies,
And 'tis this very Reason I despise: 75
This Supernatural Gift, that makes a *Mite*
Think he's the *Image* of the *Infinite*,
Comparing his short Life, void of all Rest,
To the *Eternal* and the ever Blest;
This busy, puzzling stirrer-up of doubt   80
That frames deep *Mysteries*, then finds 'em out,
Filling with frantic Crowds of thinking *Fools*
Those reverend *Bedlams, Colleges* and *Schools*;
Borne on whose wings, each heavy *Sot* can pierce
The limits of the boundless Universe;   85
So Charming Ointments make an Old *Witch* fly
And bear a Crippled Carcass through the Sky.
'Tis this exalted Pow'r, whose business lies
In *Nonsense* and *Impossibilities*,
This made a whimsical *Philosopher*   90
Before the spacious *World*, his *Tub* prefer,
And we have modern *Cloistered Coxcombs* who
Retire to think, 'cause they have nought to do.
   But thoughts are given for Action's Government;
Where Action ceases, Thought's impertinent.   95
Our *Sphere* of Action is Life's happiness,
And he who thinks beyond, thinks like an *Ass*.
Thus, whilst against false reas'ning I inveigh,
I own right *Reason*, which I would obey:
That *Reason* which distinguishes by Sense,   100
And gives us *Rules* of good and ill from thence;
That bounds Desires with a reforming Will,
To keep 'em more in vigour, not to Kill.
Your *Reason* hinders, mine helps to enjoy,

Renewing Appetites yours would destroy;   105
My Reason is my Friend, yours is a Cheat;
Hunger calls out, my Reason bids me eat;
Perversely, yours your Appetite does mock:
This asks for Food, that answers, 'What's o'Clock?'
This plain Distinction, Sir, your doubt Secures: 110
'Tis not true Reason I despise, but yours.
   'Thus I think reason righted; but for Man,
I'll ne'er Recant, defend him if you can.
For all his Pride and his Philosophy,
'Tis evident, Beasts are, in their Degree,   115
As wise at least, and better far than he.
Those Creatures are the wisest who attain,
By surest Means, the Ends at which they aim:
If therefore *Jowler* finds and kills his hares
Better than Meres supplies committee chairs,   120
Though one's a Statesman, th' other but a Hound,
Jowler, in Justice, would be wiser found.
   'You see how far Man's Wisdom here extends;
Look next if Human Nature makes amends:
Whose Principles most gen'rous are, and just,   125
And to whose Morals you would sooner trust.
Be Judge yourself, I'll bring it to the Test:
Which is the basest Creature, Man or Beast?
Birds feed on Birds, Beasts on each other prey,
But Savage Man alone does Man betray.   130
Pressed by Necessity, they Kill for Food;
Man undoes Man to do himself no good.
With Teeth and Claws by Nature Armed, they hunt
Nature's Allowance, to supply their Want.
But Man, with Smiles, Embraces, Friendship's praise,   135
Unhumanly his Fellow's Life betrays;
With voluntary Pains works his distress,
Not through Necessity, but Wantonness.
   'For Hunger or for Love they fight or tear,
Whilst wretched Man is still in Arms for fear.   140
For fear he arms, and is of Arms afraid,
By Fear to Fear successively betrayed;
Base Fear, the Source whence his best Passions came,
His boasted Honour, and his dear-bought Fame;
That Lust of Pow'r, to which he's such a Slave,   145
And for the which alone he dares be brave;
To which his various Projects are designed;
Which makes him gen'rous, affable, and kind;
For which he takes such pains to be thought wise,
And screws his Actions in a forced Disguise,   150
Leading a tedious Life in Misery
Under laborious, mean Hypocrisy.

Look to the bottom of his vast Design,
Wherein Man's Wisdom, Pow'r, and Glory join:
The Good he acts, the Ill he does endure,   155
'Tis all from fear, to make himself Secure.
Merely for Safety, after Fame we Thirst,
For all Men would be Cowards, if they durst.
    'And honesty's against all common Sense:
Men must be Knaves, 'tis in their own defence.   160
Mankind's dishonest; if you think it fair
Amongst known Cheats to play upon the Square,
You'll be undone——
Nor can weak Truth your Reputation save:
The Knaves will all agree to call you Knave.   165
Wronged shall he live, insulted o'er, oppressed,
Who dares be less a Villain than the rest.
    'Thus, Sir, you see what Human Nature craves:
Most Men are Cowards, all Men should be Knaves.
The difference lies (as far as I can see)   170
Not in the thing it self, but the degree;
And all the Subject matter of debate
Is only who's a Knave of the first Rate?
    'All this with indignation have I hurtled
At the pretending part of the proud World,   175
Who, swollen with selfish Vanity, devise
False Freedoms, holy Cheats, and formal Lies
Over their Fellow-Slaves to Tyrannize.
    'But if in Court so just a Man there be
(In Court a just Man, yet unknown to me)   180
Who does his needful flattery direct,
Not to oppress and ruin, but protect
(Since flattery, which way soever laid,
Is still a Tax on that unhappy Trade);
If so upright a States-Man you can find,   185
Whose Passions bend to his unbiased Mind,
Who does his Arts and Policies apply
To raise his Country, not his Family,
Nor, while his Pride owned Avarice withstands,
Receives close Bribes through friends' corrupted hands –   190
    'Is there a Church-Man who on God relies?
Whose Life, his Faith and Doctrine justifies?
Not one blown up with vain Prelatic Pride,
Who, for reproof of Sins, does Man deride;
Whose envious Heart makes preaching a pretence;   195
With his obstreperous, saucy Eloquence,
Dares chide at Kings, and rail at Men of Sense;
Who from his Pulpit vents more peevish Lies,
More bitter Railings, Scandals, Calumnies,
Than at a Gossiping are thrown about,   200

When the good *Wives* get drunk, and then fall out;
None of that sensual *Tribe* whose *Talents* lie
In Avarice, Pride, Sloth, and Gluttony;
Who hunt good Livings, but abhor good Lives;
Whose Lust exalted to that height arrives,   205
They act Adultery with their own *Wives*,
And ere a score of Years completed be,
Can from the lofty Pulpit proudly see
Half a large Parish their own Progeny;
   'Nor doting Bishop who would be adored   210
For domineering at the Council-Board,
A greater *Fop* in business at Fourscore,
Fonder of serious Toys, affected more,
Than the gay, glittering Fool at Twenty proves
With all his noise, his tawdry Clothes, and Loves;   215
'But a meek, humble *Man* of modest Sense,
Who, Preaching Peace, does practice Continence;
Whose pious life's a proof he does believe
Mysterious Truths, which no Man can conceive.
If upon Earth there dwell such God-like Men,   220
Then I'll Recant my Paradox to them,
Adore those *Shrines* of *Virtue*, Homage pay,
And, with the Rabble-world, their *Laws* obey.
   'If such there be, yet grant me *This* at least:
Man differs more from Man, than Man from Beast'.   225

The Disabled Debauchee

As some brave Admiral, in former War
   Deprived of Force, but pressed with Courage still,
Two Rival Fleets appearing from afar,
   Crawls to the top of an adjacent Hill,

From whence (with thoughts full of concern) he views   5
   The wise and daring Conduct of the Fight,
Whilst each bold Action to his Mind renews
   His present Glory and his past Delight;

From his fierce Eyes Flashes of Fire he throws,
   As from black Clouds when Lightning breaks away;   10
Transported, thinks himself amidst the Foes,
   And absent, yet enjoys the Bloody Day;

So, when my Days of Impotence approach,
   And I'm by Pox and Wine's unlucky Chance
Driven from the pleasing Billows of Debauch   15
   On the dull Shore of Lazy Temperance,

My pains at least some Respite shall afford
    Whilst I behold the Battles you maintain
When Fleets of Glasses sail about the Board,
    From whose Broadsides Volleys of Wit shall rain.   20

Nor let the sight of Honourable Scars,
    Which my too forward Valour did procure,
Frighten new-listed Soldiers from the Wars:
    Past joys have more than paid what I endure.

Should any Youth (worth being drunk) prove Nice,   25
    And from his fair inviter meanly shrink,
'Twill please the Ghost of my departed Vice
    If, at my counsel, he repent and drink.

Or should some cold-complexioned Sot forbid,
    With his dull morals, our Night's brisk alarms,   30
I'll fire his Blood by telling what I did
    When I was strong, and able to bear Arms.

I'll tell of Whores attacked, their Lords at home;
    Bawds' quarters beaten up, and Fortress won;
Windows demolished, Watches overcome;   35
    And handsome ills, by my contrivance done.

Nor shall our Love-fits, *Chloris*, be forgot,
    When each the well-looked Link-boy strove t' enjoy,
And the best Kiss was the deciding Lot
    Whether the Boy fucked you, or I the Boy.   40

With Tales like these, I will such Heat inspire,
    As to important Mischief shall incline;
I'll make him long some Ancient Church to fire,
    And fear no Lewdness he's called to by Wine.

Thus, Statesmanlike, I'll saucily impose,   45
    And safe from Danger, valiantly advise;
Sheltered in impotence, urge you to Blows,
    And being good for nothing else, be wise.

Lampoon [On the Women about Town]

Too long the Wise Commons have been in debate
About Money, and Conscience (those Trifles of State)
Whilst dangerous Grievances daily increase,
And the Subject can't riot in Safety and peace;
Unless (as against Irish Cattle before)   5

You now make an Act to forbid Irish whore.
The Coots (black, and white) Clenbrazell, and Fox,
Invade us with Impudence, beauty, and pox.
They carry a Fate which no man can oppose:
The loss of his heart, and the fall of his Nose.   10
Should he dully resist, yet would each take upon her,
To beseech him to do it, and engage him in honour.
O! Ye merciful powers, who of Mortals take Care,
Make the Women more modest, more sound, or less fair.
Is it just that with death cruel Love should conspire,   15
And our Tarses be burnt by our hearts taking fire?
There's an end of Communion if humble Believers
Must be damned in the Cup like unworthy Receivers.

Signior Dildo

You Ladies all of Merry England
Who have been to kiss the Duchess's hand,
Pray did you lately observe in the Show
A Noble Italian called Signior Dildo?

The Signior was one of her Highness's Train   5
And helped to Conduct her over the Main,
But now she Cries out to the Duke, 'I will go,
I have no more need for Signior Dildo'.

At the Sign of the Cross in Saint James's Street,
When next you go thither to make your Selves Sweet,   10
By Buying of Powder, Gloves, Essence, or So
You may Chance get a Sight of Signior Dildo.

You'll take him at first for no Person of Note
Because he appears in a plain Leather Coat:
But when you his virtuous Abilities know   15
You'll fall down and Worship Signior Dildo.

My Lady Southesk, Heav'ns prosper her for 't
First Clothed him in Satin, then brought him to Court;
But his Head in the Circle, he Scarcely durst Show,
So modest a Youth was Signior Dildo.   20

The good Lady Suffolk thinking no harm
Had got this poor Stranger hid under her Arm:
Lady Betty by Chance came the Secret to know,
And from her own Mother, Stole Signior Dildo:

The Countess of Falmouth, of whom People tell   25
Her Footmen wear Shirts of a Guinea an Ell:
Might Save the Expense, if she did but know
How Lusty a Swinger is Signior Dildo.

By the Help of this Gallant the Countess of Rafe
Against the fierce Harris preserved her Self Safe: 30
She Stifled him almost beneath her Pillow,
So Closely she embraced Signior Dildo.

Our dainty fine Duchesses have got a Trick
To Dote on a Fool, for the Sake of his Prick,
The Fops were undone, did their Graces but know   35
The Discretion and vigour of Signior Dildo.

That Pattern of Virtue, her Grace of Cleveland,
Has Swallowed more Pricks, than the Ocean has Sand,
But by Rubbing and Scrubbing, so large it does grow,
It is fit for just nothing but Signior Dildo.   40

The Duchess of Modena, though she looks high,
With such a Gallant is contented to Lie:
And for fear the English her Secrets should know,
For a Gentleman Usher took Signior Dildo.

The countess of the Cockpit (who knows not her Name?)   45
She's famous in Story for a Killing Dame:
When all her old Lovers forsake her I Trow
She'll then be contented with Signior Dildo.

Red Howard, Red Sheldon, and Temple so tall
Complain of his absence so long from Whitehall: 50
Signior Barnard has promised a Journey to go,
And bring back his Countryman Signior Dildo.

Doll Howard no longer with his Highness must Range,
And therefore is proffered this Civil Exchange:
Her Teeth being rotten, she Smells best below,   55
And needs must be fitted for Signior Dildo

St Albans with Wrinkles and Smiles in his Face
Whose kindness to Strangers, becomes his high Place,
In his Coach and Six Horses is gone to Pergo
To take the fresh Air with Signior Dildo.   60

Were this Signior but known to the Citizen Fops
He'd keep their fine Wives from the Foremen of Shops,

But the Rascals deserve their Horns should still grow,
For Burning the Pope, and his Nephew Dildo.

Tom Killigrew's wife, North Holland's fine Flower,   65
At the Sight of this Signior, did fart, and Belch Sour,
And her Dutch Breeding further to Show,
Says 'welcome to England, myn Heer Van Dildo'.

He civilly came to the Cockpit one night,
And proffered his Service to fair Madam Knight,   70
Quoth she, 'I intrigue with Captain Cazzo.
Your Nose in myne Arse good Signior Dildo'.

This Signior is sound, safe, ready, and Dumb,
As ever was Candle, Carrot, or Thumb:
Then away with these nasty devices, and Show   75
How you rate the just merits of Signior Dildo.

Count Cazzo who carries his Nose very high,
In Passion he Swore, his Rival should Die,
Then Shut up himself, to let the world know,
Flesh and Blood could not bear it from Signior Dildo.   80

A Rabble of Pricks, who were welcome before,
Now finding the Porter denied 'em the Door,
Maliciously waited his coming below,
And inhumanely fell on Signior Dildo.

Nigh wearied out, the poor Stranger did fly
And along the Pall Mall, they followed full Cry   85
The Women concerned from every Window,
Cried, 'Oh! for Heav'n's sake save Signior Dildo'.

The good Lady Sandys, burst into a Laughter
To see how the Ballocks came wobbling after,   90
And had not their weight retarded the Foe
Indeed 't had gone hard with Signior Dildo.

A Satyr on Charles II

In th' Isle of Britain, long since famous grown
For breeding the best cunts in Christendom,
There reigns, and oh long may he reign and thrive
The easiest King and best bred man alive.
Him no Ambition moves, to get Renown   5
Like the french Fool, hazarding his Crown.
Peace is his Aim, his Gentleness is such

And Love, he loves, for he loves fucking much.
Nor are his high Desires above his Strength:
His Sceptre and his Prick are of a Length;   10
And she may sway the one, who plays with th' other
And make him little wiser than his Brother.
Restless he rolls about from Whore to Whore
A merry Monarch, scandalous and poor.
Poor Prince thy Prick like thy Buffoons at Court   15
Will govern thee because it makes thee sport.
'Tis sure the sauciest that e'er did swive
The proudest, peremptoriest Prick alive.
Though Safety, Law, Religion, Life lay on 't,
'Twould break through all to make its way to Cunt.   20
To Carwell the most Dear of all his dears
The best Relief of his declining years
Oft he bewails his fortune, and her fate
To love so well and be beloved so late.
For though in her he settles well his Tarse   25
Yet his dull graceless Ballocks hang an arse.
This you'd believe had I but Time to tell you
The Pains it Costs the poor laborious Nelly
Whilst she employs, hands, fingers, mouth, and thighs
Ere she can raise the Member she enjoys –   30
I hate all Monarchs, and the Thrones they sit on
From the Hector of France to the Cully of Britain.

A Letter from Artemiza in the Town
to Chloe in the Country

Chloe, in Verse by your command I write;
Shortly you'll bid me ride astride, and fight.
These Talents better with our sex agree,
Than lofty flights of dang'rous poetry.
Amongst the Men (I mean) the Men of Wit   5
(At least they passed for such, before they writ)
How many bold Advent'rers for the Bays,
(Proudly designing large returns of praise)
Who durst that stormy pathless World explore,
Were soon dashed back, and wrecked on the dull shore,   10
Broke of that little stock, they had before?
How would a Woman's tott'ring Bark be tossed,
Where stoutest Ships (the Men of Wit) are lost?
When I reflect on this, I straight grow wise,
And my own self thus gravely I advise.   15
Dear Artemiza, poetry's a snare:
Bedlam has many Mansions: have a Care.

Your Muse diverts you, makes the Reader sad;
You fancy, you're inspired, he thinks you mad.
Consider too, 'twill be discreetly done,   20
To make your Self the Fiddle of the Town,
To find th' ill-humored pleasure at their need,
Cursed, if you fail, and scorned, though you succeed.
Thus, like an Arrant Woman, as I am,
No sooner well convinced, writing's a shame,   25
That Whore is scarce a more reproachful name,
Than poetess:
Like Men, that marry, or like Maids, that woo,
'Cause 'tis the very worst thing they can do,
Pleased with the Contradiction, and the Sin,   30
Mee-thinks, I stand on Thorns, till I begin.
Y' expect at least, to hear, what Loves have past
In this Lewd Town, since you, and I met last.
What change has happened of Intrigues, and whether
The Old ones last, and who, and who's together.   35
But how, my dearest Chloe, shall I set
My pen to write, what I would fain forget,
Or name that lost thing (Love) without a tear
Since so debauched by ill-bred Customs here?
Love, the most generous passion of the mind,   40
The softest refuge Innocence can find,
The safe director of unguided youth,
Fraught with kind wishes, and secured by Truth,
That Cordial drop Heav'n in our Cup has thrown,
To make the nauseous draught of life go down,   45
On which one only blessing God might raise
In lands of Atheists Subsidies of praise
(For none did e'er so dull, and stupid prove,
But felt a God, and blest his power in Love)
This only Joy, for which poor We were made,   50
Is grown like play, to be an Arrant Trade;
The Rooks creep in, and it has got of late
As many little Cheats, and Tricks, as that.
But what yet more a Woman's heart would vex,
'Tis chiefly carried on by our own Sex,   55
Our silly Sex, who born, like Monarchs, free,
Turn Gypsies for a meaner Liberty,
And hate restraint, though but from Infamy.
They call whatever is not Common, nice,
And deaf to Nature's rule, or Love's advice,   60
Forsake the pleasure, to pursue the vice.
To an exact perfection they have wrought
The Action Love, the Passion is forgot.
'Tis below wit, they tell you, to admire,
And ev'n without approving they desire.   65

Their private wish obeys the public Voice,
'Twixt good, and bad Whimsy decides, not Choice.
Fashions grow up for taste, at Forms they strike:
They know, what they would have, not what they like.
Bovey's a beauty, if some few agree,   70
To call him so, the rest to that degree
Affected are, that with their Ears they see.
Where I was visiting the other night,
Comes a fine Lady with her humble Knight,
Who had prevailed on her, through her own skill,   75
At his request, though much against his will,
To come to London.
As the Coach stopped, we heard her Voice more loud,
Than a great bellied Woman's in a Crowd,
Telling the Knight, that her affairs require,   80
He for some hours obsequiously retire.
I think, she was ashamed, to have him seen
(Hard fate of Husbands) the Gallant had been,
Though a diseased ill-favoured Fool, brought in.
'Dispatch', says she, 'that business you pretend,   85
Your beastly visit to your drunken friend;
A Bottle ever makes you look so fine!
Methinks I long to smell you stink of Wine.
Your Country-drinking-breath's enough to kill
Sour Ale corrected with a Lemon peel.   90
Prithee farewell – we'll meet again anon';
The necessary thing bows, and is gone.
She flies up stairs, and all the haste does show,
That fifty Antic Postures will allow,
And then bursts out – 'Dear madam, am not I   95
The alter'dst Creature breathing? Let me die,
I find myself ridiculously grown
Embarrassée with being out of Town,
Rude, and untaught, like any Indian Queen;
My Country nakedness is strangely seen.   100
How is Love governed? Love, that rules the State,
And, pray, who are the Men most worn of late?
When I was married, Fools were *à la mode*,
The Men of Wit were then held *incommode*,
Slow of belief, and fickle in desire,   105
Who ere they'll be persuaded, must inquire,
As if they came to spy, not to admire.
With searching Wisdom fatal to their ease
They still find out, why, what may, should not please;
Nay take themselves for injured, when We dare,   110
Make 'em think better of us, than We are:
And if We hide our frailties from their sights,
Call Us deceitful Jilts and Hypocrites.

They little guess, who at Our Arts are grieved,
The perfect Joy of being well deceived.   115
Inquisitive, as jealous Cuckolds, grow,
Rather than not be knowing, they will know,
What being known creates their certain woe.
Women should these of all mankind avoid;
For Wonder by clear knowledge is destroyed.   120
Woman, who is an Arrant Bird of night,
Bold in the Dusk, before a Fool's dull sight,
Should fly, when Reason brings the glaring light:
But the kind easy Fool apt to admire
Himself, trusts us, his Follies all conspire,   125
To flatter his, and favour Our desire.
Vain of his proper Merit he with ease
Believes, we love him best, who best can please.
On him Our gross dull common Flatteries pass,
Ever most Joyful, when most made an Ass.   130
Heavy, to apprehend, though all Mankind
Perceive Us false, the Fop concerned is blind,
Who doting on himself,
Thinks every one, that sees him, of his mind.
These are true women's Men'. – Here forced to cease   135
Through Want of Breath, not Will, to hold her peace,
She to the Window runs, where she had spied
Her much esteemed dear Friend the monkey tied.
With forty smiles, as many Antic bows,
As if 't had been the Lady of the House,   140
The dirty chattering Monster she embraced,
And made it this fine tender speech at last
'Kiss me, thou curious Miniature of Man;
How odd thou art? How pretty? How Japan?
Oh I could live, and die with thee' – then on   145
For half an hour in Compliment she run.
I took this time, to think, what Nature meant,
When this mixed thing into the World she sent,
So very wise, yet so impertinent.
One, who knew every thing, who, God thought fit,   150
Should be an Ass through choice, not want of Wit:
Whose Foppery, without the help of Sense,
Could ne'er have rose to such an Excellence.
Nature's as lame, in making a true Fop,
As a Philosopher; the very top,   155
And Dignity of Folly we attain
By studious Search, and labour of the Brain,
By observation, Counsel, and deep thought:
God never made a Coxcomb worth a groat.
We owe that name to Industry, and Arts: 160
An Eminent Fool must be a Fool of parts;

And such a one was she, who had turned o'er
As many Books, as Men, loved much, read more,
Had a discerning Wit; to her was known
Every one's fault, and merit, but her own.   165
All the good qualities, that ever blest
A Woman, so distinguished from the rest,
Except discretion only, she possessed.
But now, '*Mon cher* dear Pug', she cries, '*adieu*',
And the Discourse broke off does thus renew.   170
'You smile, to see me, whom the World perchance
Mistakes, to have some Wit, so far advance
The interest of Fools, that I approve
Their Merit more, than Men's of Wit, in Love.
But in Our Sex too many proofs there are   175
Of such, whom Wits undo, and Fools repair.
This in my time was so observed a Rule,
Hardly a Wench in Town, but had her Fool.
The meanest Common Slut, who long was grown
The Jest, and Scorn of every Pit-Buffon,   180
Had yet left Charms enough, to have subdued
Some Fop, or other fond, to be thought lewd.
Foster could make an Irish Lord a Nokes,
And Betty Morris had her City-Cokes.
A Woman's ne'er so ruined, but she can   185
Be still revenged on her undoer Man.
How lost so e'er, she'll find some Lover more
A lewd abandoned Fool, than she a whore.
That wretched thing Corinna, who had run
Through all the several Ways of being undone,   190
Cozened at first by Love, and living then
By turning the too-dear-bought trick on Men:
Gay were the hours, and winged with Joys they flew,
When first the Town her early Beauties knew,
Courted, admired, and loved, with presents fed,   195
Youth in her looks, and pleasure in her bed,
Till Fate, or her ill Angel thought it fit,
To make her dote upon a Man of Wit,
Who found, 'twas dull, to love above a day,
Made his ill-natured Jest, and went away.   200
Now scorned by all, forsaken, and oppressed,
She's a *Memento Mori* to the rest.
Diseased, decayed, to take up half a Crown,
Must mortgage her long Scarf, and Manteau Gown.
Poor Creature! Who unheard of, as a Fly,   205
In some dark hole must all the Winter lie,
And Want, and dirt endure a whole half year,
That for one Month she tawdry may appear.
In Easter Term she gets her a new Gown,

When my young Master's Worship comes to Town,   210
From Pedagogue, and Mother just set free,
The Heir, and Hopes of a great Family,
Which with strong Ale, and Beef the Country Rules,
And ever since the Conquest have been Fools:
And now with careful prospect to maintain   215
This Character, lest crossing of the Strain
Should mend the Booby-breed, his Friends provide
A cousin of his own, to be his Bride;
And thus set out –
With an Estate, no Wit, and a young Wife   220
(The solid comforts of a Coxcomb's life)
Dunghill, and Pease forsook, he comes to Town,
Turns Spark, learns to be lewd, and is undone.
Nothing suits worse with Vice than want of Sense,
Fools are still wicked at their own Expense.   225
This o'ergrown Schoolboy lost – Corinna wins,
And at first dash, to make an Ass, begins:
Pretends, to like a Man, who has not known
The Vanities, nor Vices of the Town,
Fresh in his youth, and faithful in his Love;   230
Eager of Joys, which he does seldom prove,
Healthful, and strong, he does no pains endure,
But what the Fair One, he adores, can cure.
Grateful for favours does the Sex esteem,
And libels none, for being kind to him.   235
Then of the Lewdness of the times complains,
Rails at the Wits, and Atheists, and maintains,
'Tis better, than good Sense, than power, or Wealth,
To have a love untainted, youth, and health.
The unbred puppy, who had never seen   240
A Creature look so gay, or talk so fine,
Believes, then falls in Love, and then in Debt,
Mortgages all, ev'n to th' Ancient Seat,
To buy this Mistress a new house for life;
To give her Plate, and Jewels, robs his wife;   245
And when to th' height of fondness he is grown,
'Tis time, to poison him, and all's her own.
Thus meeting in her Common Arms his Fate,
He leaves her Bastard Heir to his Estate;
And as the Race of such an Owl deserves,   250
His own dull lawful progeny he starves.
Nature, who never made a thing in vain,
But does each Insect to some end ordain,
Wisely contrived kind-keeping Fools, no doubt,
To patch up Vices, Men of Wit wear out'   255
Thus she ran on two hours, some grains of Sense
Still mixed with Volleys of Impertinence.

But now 'tis time, I should some pity show
To Chloe, since I cannot choose, but know,
Readers must reap the dullness writers sow.   260
By the next Post such stories I will tell,
As joined with these shall to a volume swell,
As true, as Heaven, more infamous than Hell;
But you are tired, and so am I. Farewell.

A Ramble in Saint James's Park

Much wine had past with grave discourse
Of who Fucks who and who does worse
Such as you usually do hear
From those that diet at the *Beare*
When I who still take care to see   5
Drunkenness Reliev'd by Lechery
Went out into Saint James's Park
To coole my head and fire my heart.
But tho' Saint James has the Honor on't
'Tis Consecrate to Prick and Cunt.   ·10
There by a most incestuous Birth
Strange woods spring from the Teeming Earth
For they Relate how heretofore
When ancient Pict began to whore
Deluded of his Assignation   15
(Jylting it seems was then in fashion)
Poor pensive Lover in this place
Wou'd frigg upon his Mothers face
Whence Rowes of Mandrakes tall did rise
Whose lewd Tops Fuckt the very Skies   20
Each imitative branch does twine
In some lov'd fold of Aretine
And nightly now beneath their shade
Are Buggeries, Rapes, and Incests made:
Unto this all-sin-sheltring Grove   25
Whores of the Bulk, and the Alcove,
Great Ladies, Chamber Mayds, and Drudges,
The Rag picker, and Heiress Trudges;
Carrmen, Divines, Great Lords, and Taylors,
Prentices, Poets, Pimps, and Gaolers,   30
Footmen, Fine Fops, doe here arrive,
And here promiscuously they swive.
Along these hallow'd walkes it was
That I beheld *Corinna* pass.
Who ever had been by to see   35
The proud disdain she cast on Me
Through charming eies he would have swore

She dropt from Heaven that very Hour
Forsakeing the Divine abode
In scorn of some dispairing God.   40
But mark what Creatures women are
How infinitely vile when fair:
Three Knights of the Elboe and the Slurr
With wriggling tails made up to her.
   The first was of your *Whitehall* Blades   45
Nere kin to the Mother of the Mayds
Grac'd by whose favor he was able
To bring a Friend to the waiters Table
Where he had heard *Sir Edward Sutton*
Say how the *King* lov'd *Banstead* Mutton;   50
Since when he'd nere be brought to eat
By's good will any other meat.
In this as well as all the rest
He ventures to doe like the best
But wanting Common Sense, th' ingredient   55
In choosing well not least expedient
Converts abortive Imitation
To universall Affectation.
Thus he not only eats and Talks
But feels and smells sits down and walks   60
Nay looks, and lives, and loves by Rote
In an old Tawdry Birthday Coat.
   The second was a Grays Inn wit
A great Inhabiter of the Pit
Where Critick-like he sitts and squints   65
Steales Pockett Handkerchefs and hints
From's Neighbour and the Comedy
To Court and pay his Landlady.
   The third a Ladys Eldest Son
Within few yeares of Twenty one   70
Who hopes from his propitious Fate
Against he comes to his Estate
By these Two Worthies to be made
A most accomplish'd tearing blade.
   One in a strain 'twixt Tune and Nonsense   75
Cries Madam I have lov'd you long since
Permitt me your fair hand to kiss;
When at her Mouth her Cunt cries yes.
In short without much more adoe
Joyfull and pleas'd away she flew   80
And with these Three Confounded Asses
From Park to Hackney Coach she passes.
   So a proud Bitch does lead about
Of humble Curs the Amorous Rout
Who most obsequiously doe hunt   85

The savory scent of salt swoln Cunt.
Some power more patient now Relate
The sence of this surprising Fate.
Gods! that a thing admir'd by mee
Shou'd fall to so much Infamy.   90
Had she pickt out to rub her Arse on
Some stiff prickt Clown or well hung Parson
Each jobb of whose spermatique sluce
Had fill'd her Cunt with wholesome Juice
I the proceeding should have praisd   95
In hope she had quench'd a fire I rais'd.
Such naturall freedoms are but Just
There's something Genrous in meer lust.
But to turn damn'd abandon'd Jade
When neither Head nor Tail perswade   100
To be a Whore in understanding
A passive pot for Fools to spend in.
The Devill play'd booty sure with Thee
To bring a blot on Infamy.
But why am I of all Mankind   105
To so severe a Fate design'd
Ungratefull! Why this Treachery
To humble fond beleiveing mee
Who gave you Privilege above
The nice allowances of Love?   110
Did ever I refuse to bear
The meanest part your Lust could spare
When your lewd Cunt came spewing home
Drench't with the seed of half the Town
My dram of sperm was sup't up after   115
For the digestive surfeit water.
Full gorged at another time
With a vast meal of nasty slime
Which your devouring Cunt had drawn
From Porters Backs and Footmens brawn   120
I was content to serve you up
My Ballock full for your Grace cup
Nor ever thought it an abuse
While you had pleasure for excuse
You that cou'd make my heart away   125
For noise and Colour and betray
The secretts of my tender houres
To such knight errant Paramours
When leaning on your faithless breast
Wrapt in security and rest   130
Soft kindness all my powers did move
And Reason lay dissolv'd in Love.
     May stinking vapours Choak your womb

Such as the Men you doat upon
May your depraved Appetite   135
That cou'd in whiffling Fools delight
Beget such Frenzies in your Mind
You may goe mad for the North wind
And fixing all your hopes upont
To have him bluster in your Cunt   140
Turn up your longing Arse to the Air
And perish in a wild dispair.
   But Cowards shall forgett to rant,
School-Boyes to Frigg, old whores to paint;
The Jesuits Fraternity   145
Shall leave the use of Buggery;
Crab-louse inspir'd with Grace divine
From Earthly Codd to Heaven shall climb;
Phisitions shall believe in Jesus
And Disobedience cease to please us   150
E're I desist with all my Power
To plague this woman and undo her.
But my Revenge will best be tim'd
When she is Married, that is lym'd.
In that most lamentable state   155
I'le make her feel my scorn and hate
Pelt her with scandalls, Truth or lies
And her poor Cur with Jealousies
Till I have torn him from her Breech
While she whines like a Dog-drawn Bitch   160
Loath'd, and despis'd, Kick't out of Town
Into some dirty Hole alone
To chew the Cud of Misery
And know she owes it all to Mee.
   And may no Woman better thrive   165
   That dares prophane the Cunt I swive.

Song

Fair *Cloris* in a Piggsty lay
   Her tender herd lay by her
She slept; in murm'ring Gruntlings they
Complayneing of the scorching Day
   Her slumbers thus inspire.   5

She dreamt while she with carefull pains
   Her snowy Arms employ'd
In Ivory pailes to fill out graines
One of her Love Convicted Swaines
   Thus hasting to her cry'd.   10

Fly *Nymph* oh! fly ere 'tis too late
    A Dear lov'd Life to save
Rescue your bosom Pigg from fate
Who now expires hung in the Gate
    That leads to Floras Cave.   15

My selfe had try'd to sett him free
    Rather then brought the newes
But I am so abhorr'd by Thee
That even thy darlings Life from Me
    I know thou wouldst refuse.   20

Struck with the news as quick she flies
    As blushes to her face
Not the bright Lightning from the Skies
Nor Love shott from her brighter eies
    Move halfe so swift a pace.   25

This Plott it seems the Lustfull Slave
    Had layd against her Honor
Which not one God took care to save
For he pursues her to the Cave
    And throwes him selfe upon her.   30

Now peirced is her virgin Zone
    She feels the Foe within it
She heares a broken Amorous groan
The panting Lovers fainting moan
    Just in the happy minute.   35

Frighted she wakes and wakeing Frigs
    Nature thus kindly eas'd
In dreams rais'd by her murmring Piggs
And her own Thumb between her legs
    She's Innocent and pleas'd.   40

A Song

1

Absent from thee I languish still,
    Then ask me not, when I return?
The straying Fool 'twill plainly kill,
    To wish all Day, all Night to Mourn.

2

Dear; from thine Arms then let me flie,   5
    That my Fantastick mind may prove,

The Torments it deserves to try,
    That tears my fixt Heart from my Love.

3
When wearied with a world of Woe,
    To thy safe Bosom I retire   10
Where Love and Peace and Truth does flow,
    May I contented there expire.

4
Lest once more wandring from that Heav'n
    I fall on some base heart unblest;
Faithless to thee, False, unforgiv'n,   15
    And lose my Everlasting rest.

Jonathan Swift
(1667–1745)

A Description of the Morning

Now hardly here and there a Hackney-coach
Appearing, showed the ruddy Morn's approach.
Now *Betty* from her Master's Bed had flown,
And softly stole to discompose her own.
The Slip-shod 'Prentice from his master's door   5
Had pared the street, and sprinkled round the floor
Now *Moll* had whirled her Mop with dext'rous Airs,
Prepared to scrub the Entry and the Stairs.
The youth with broomy stumps began to trace
The kennel edge, where wheels had worn the place.   10
The Small-coal Man was heard with Cadence deep,
Till drowned in shriller Notes of *Chimney Sweep*.
Duns at his lordship's gate began to meet;
And brickdust-*Moll* had screamed through half a Street.
The Turnkey now his flock Returning sees,   15
Duly let out a-Nights to steal for Fees.
The watchful Bailiffs take their silent Stands;
And Schoolboys lag with Satchels in their Hands.

A Description of a City Shower

Careful Observers may foretell the Hour
By sure Prognostics when to dread a Show'r:
While Rain depends, the pensive Cat gives o'er
Her Frolics, and pursues her Tail no more.
Returning Home at Night, you find the Sink   5
Strike your offended Sense with double Stink.
If you be wise, then go not far to dine:
You spend in Coach-hire more than save in Wine.
A coming Show'r your shooting Corns presage;
Old Aches throb, your hollow Tooth will rage: 10
A Saunt'ring in Coffee-house is *Dulman* seen;
He damns the Climate, and complains of Spleen.
Mean while the South, rising with dabbled Wings,
A sable Cloud athwart the Welkin flings

That swilled more Liquor than it could contain,   15
And, like a Drunkard, gives it up again.
Brisk *Susan* whips her Linen from the Rope,
While the first drizzling Show'r is borne aslope:
Such is that Sprinkling, which some careless Quean
Flirts on you from her Mop; but not so clean: 20
You fly, invoke the Gods; then turning, stop
To rail; she singing still whirls on her Mop.
Nor yet the Dust had shunned th' unequal Strife,
But, aided by the Wind, fought still for Life;
And wafted with its Foe by violent Gust,   25
'Twas doubtful which was Rain, and which was Dust,
Ah! where must needy Poet seek for Aid,
When Dust and Rain at once his Coat invade?
Sole Coat, where Dust cemented by the Rain,
Erects the Nap, and leaves a cloudy Stain.   30
Now, in contiguous Drops the Flood comes down,
Threat'ning with Deluge this *devoted* Town.
To Shops in Crowds the daggled Females fly,
Pretend to cheapen Goods, but nothing buy.
The Templer spruce, while every Spout's abroach,   35
Stays till 'tis fair, yet *seems* to call a Coach.
The tucked-up Sempstress walks with hasty Strides,
While Streams run down her oil'd Umbrella's Sides.
Here various Kinds, by various Fortunes led,
Commence Acquaintance underneath a Shed: 40
Triumphant Tories, and desponding Whigs,
Forget their Feuds, and join to save their Wigs.
Boxed in a Chair the Beau impatient sits,
While Spouts run clatt'ring o'er the Roof by Fits,
And ever and anon with frightful Din   45
The Leather sounds; he trembles from within.
So when *Troy* Chairmen bore the wooden Steed,
Pregnant with *Greeks*, impatient to be freed;
(Those Bully *Greeks*, who, as the Moderns do,
Instead of paying Chair-men, run them through)   50
Laocoon struck the Outside with his Spear,
And each imprisoned Hero quaked for Fear.
   Now from all Parts the swelling Kennels flow,
And bear their Trophies with them, as they go:
Filths of all Hues and Odours seem to tell   55
What Street they sailed from, by the Sight and Smell.
They, as each Torrent drives with rapid Force,
From *Smithfield*, or *St. Pulchre*'s shape their course,
And in huge Confluent joined at *Snow-hill* Ridge,
Fall from the *Conduit* prone to *Holborn-Bridge*.   60
Sweepings from Butchers' Stalls, Dung, Guts, and Blood,

Drowned Puppies, stinking Sprats, all drenched in Mud,
Dead Cats, and Turnip-Tops come tumbling down the Flood.

Strephon and *Chloe*

Of *Chloe* all the Town has rung;
By ev'ry size of Poets sung:
So beautiful a Nymph appears
But once in Twenty Thousand Years.
By Nature form'd with nicest Care,   5
And, faultless to a single Hair.
Her graceful Mein, her Shape, and Face,
Confest her of no mortal Race:
And then, so nice, and so genteel;
Such Cleanliness from Head to Heel: 10
No Humours gross, or frowzy Steams,
No noisom Whiffs, or sweaty Streams,
Before, behind, above, below,
Could from her taintless Body flow.
Would so discreetly Things dispose,   15
None ever saw her pluck a Rose.
Her dearest Comrades never caught her
Squat on her Hams, to make Maid's Water.
You'd swear, that so divine a Creature
Felt no Necessities of Nature.   20
In Summer had she walkt the Town,
Her Armpits would not stain her Gown:
At Country Dances, not a Nose
Could in the Dog-Days smell her Toes.
Her Milk-white Hands, both Palms and Backs,   25
Like Iv'ry dry, and soft as Wax.
Her Hands the softest ever felt,
Tho' cold would burn, tho' dry would melt.
     DEAR *Venus*, hide this wond'rous Maid,
Nor let her loose to spoil your Trade.   30
While she engrosseth ev'ry Swain,
You but o'er half the World can reign.
Think what a Case all Men are now in,
What ogling, sighing, toasting, vowing!
What powder'd Wigs! What Flames and Darts!   35
What Hampers full of bleeding Hearts!
What Sword-knots! What Poetic Strains!
What Billet-doux, and clouded Cains!
     BUT, *Strephon* sigh'd so loud and strong,
He blew a Settlement along: 40
And, bravely drove his Rivals down

With Coach and Six, and House in Town.
The bashful Nymph no more withstands,
Because her dear Papa commands.
The charming Couple now unites;   45
Proceed we to the Marriage Rites.
    IMPRIMIS, at the Temple Porch
Stood *Hymen* with a flaming Torch.
The smiling *Cyprian* Goddess brings
Her infant Loves with purple Wings;   50
And Pigeons billing, Sparrows treading,
Fair Emblems of a fruitful Wedding.
The Muses next in Order follow,
Conducted by their Squire, *Apollo:*
Then *Mercury* with Silver Tongue,   55
And *Hebe,* Goddess ever young.
Behold the Bridegroom and his Bride,
Walk Hand in Hand, and Side by Side;
She by the tender Graces drest,
But, he by *Mars,* in Scarlet Vest.   60
The Nymph was cover'd with her *Flammeum,*
And *Phœbus* sung th' *Epithalamium.*
And, last to make the Matter sure,
Dame *Juno* brought a Priest demure.
Luna was absent on Pretence   65
Her Time was not till Nine Months hence.
    THE Rites perform'd, the Parson paid,
In State return'd the grand Parade;
With loud Huzza's from all the Boys,
That now the Pair must *crown their joys.*   70
    BUT, still the hardest Part remains.
Strephon had long perplex'd his Brains,
How with so high a Nymph he might
Demean himself the Wedding-Night:
For, as he view'd his Person round,   75
Meer mortal Flesh was all he found:
His Hand, his Neck, his Mouth, and Feet
Were duly washt to keep 'em sweet;
(With other Parts that shall be nameless,
The Ladies else might think me shameless.)   80
The Weather and his Love were hot;
And should he struggle; I know what—
Why let it go, if I must tell it—
He'll sweat, and then the Nymph may smell it.
While she a Goddess dy'd in Grain   85
Was unsusceptible of Stain:
And, *Venus*-like, her fragrant Skin
Exhal'd *Ambrosia* from within:
Can such a Deity endure

A mortal human Touch impure?   90
How did the humbled Swain detest
His prickled Beard, and hairy Breast!
His Night-Cap border'd round with Lace
Could give no Softness to his Face.

    YET, if the Goddess could be kind,   95
What endless Raptures must he find!
And Goddesses have now and then
Come down to visit mortal Men:
To visit and to court them too;
A certain Goddess, God knows who,   100
(As in a Book he heard it read)
Took Col'nel *Peleus* to her Bed.
But, what if he should lose his Life
By vent'ring *on* his heav'nly Wife?
For *Strephon* could remember well,   105
That, once he heard a Schoolboy tell,
How *Semele* of mortal Race,
By Thunder dy'd in *Jove's* Embrace;
And what if daring *Strephon* dies
By Lightning shot from *Chloe's* Eyes?   110

    WHILE these Reflections fill'd his Head,
The Bride was put in Form to Bed;
He follow'd, stript, and in he crept,
But, awfully his Distance kept.

    Now, *Ponder well ye Parents dear,*   115
Forbid your Daughters guzzling Beer;
And make them ev'ry Afternoon
Forbear their Tea, or drink it soon;
That, e'er to Bed they venture up,
They may discharge it ev'ry Sup;   120
If not; they must in evil Plight
Be often forc'd to rise at Night,
Keep them to wholsome Food confin'd,
Nor let them taste what causes Wind;
('Tis this the Sage of *Samos* means,   125
Forbidding his Disciples Beans)
O, think what Evils must ensue;
Miss *Moll* the Jade will burn it blue:
And when she once has got the Art,
She cannot help it for her Heart;   130
But, out it flies, even when she meets
Her Bridegroom in the Wedding-Sheets.
Carminative and *Diuretic*,
Will damp all Passion Sympathetic;
And, Love such Nicety requires,   135
One *Blast* will put out all his Fires.
Since Husbands get behind the Scene,

The Wife should study to be clean;
Nor give the smallest Room to guess
The Time when Wants of Nature press;   140
    BUT, after Marriage, practise more
Decorum than she did before;
To keep her Spouse deluded still,
And make him fancy what she will.
    IN Bed we left the married Pair;   145
'Tis Time to shew how Things went there.
Strephon, who had been often told,
That Fortune still assists the bold,
Resolv'd to make his first Attack:
But, *Chloe* drove him fiercely back.   150
How could a Nymph so chaste as *Chloe*,
With Constitution cold and snowy,
Permit a brutish Man to touch her?
Ev'n Lambs by Instinct fly the Butcher.
Resistance on the Wedding-Night   155
Is what our Maidens claim by Right:
And, *Chloe*, 'tis by all agreed,
Was Maid in Thought, and Word, and Deed,
Yet, some assign a diff'rent Reason;
That *Strephon* chose no proper Season.   160
    SAY, fair ones, must I make a Pause?
Or freely tell the secret Cause.
    TWELVE Cups of Tea, (with Grief I speak)
Had now constrain'd the Nymph to leak.
This Point must needs be settled first;   165
The Bride must either void or burst.
Then, see the dire Effect of Pease,
Think what can give the Colick Ease,
The Nymph opprest before, behind,
As Ships are toss't by Waves and Wind,   170
Steals out her Hand by Nature led,
And brings a Vessel into Bed:
Fair Utensil, as smooth and white
As *Chloe*'s Skin, almost as bright.
    STREPHON who heard the fuming Rill   175
As from a mossy Cliff distill;
Cry'd out, ye Gods, what Sound is this?
Can *Chloe*, heav'nly *Chloe*—?
But, when he smelt a noysom Steam
Which oft attends that luke-warm Stream;   180
(*Salerno* both together joins
As sov'reign Med'cines for the Loins)
And, though contriv'd, we may suppose
To slip his Ears, yet struck his Nose:
He found her, while the Scent increas'd,   185

As *mortal* as himself at least.
But, soon with like Occasions prest,
He boldly sent his Hand in quest
(Inspir'd with Courage from his Bride),
To reach the Pot on t' other Side.   190
And as he fill'd the reeking Vase,
Let fly a Rouzer in her Face.
   THE little *Cupids* hov'ring round,
(As Pictures prove) with Garlands crown'd,
Abasht at what they saw and heard,   195
Flew off, nor evermore appear'd.
   ADIEU to ravishing Delights,
High Raptures, and romantick Flights;
To Goddesses so heav'nly sweet,
Expiring Shepherds at their Feet;   200
To silver Meads, and shady Bow'rs,
Drest up with *Amaranthine* Flow'rs.
   How great a Change! how quickly made!
They learn to call a Spade, a Spade.
They soon from all Constraint are freed;   205
Can see each other *do their Need*.
On Box of Cedar sits the Wife,
And makes it warm for *Dearest Life*.
And, by the beastly way of Thinking,
Find great Society in Stinking.   210
Now *Strephon* daily entertains
His *Chloe* in the homeliest Strains;
And, *Chloe* more experienc'd grown,
With Int'rest pays him back his own.
No Maid at Court is less asham'd,   215
Howe'er for selling Bargains fam'd,
Than she, to name her Parts behind,
Or when a-bed, to let out Wind.
   FAIR *Decency*, celestial Maid,
Descend from Heav'n to Beauty's Aid;   220
Though Beauty may beget Desire,
'Tis thou must fan the Lover's Fire;
For, Beauty, like supreme Dominion,
Is best supported by Opinion;
If Decency brings no Supplies,   225
Opinion falls, and Beauty dies.
   To see some radiant Nymph appear
In all her glitt'ring Birthday Gear,
You think some Goddess from the Sky
Descended, ready cut and dry: 230
But, e'er you sell your self to Laughter,
Consider well what may come after;
For fine Ideas vanish fast,

While all the gross and filthy last.
    O *Strephon*, e'er that fatal Day   235
When *Chloe* stole your Heart away,
Had you but through a Cranny spy'd
On House of Ease your future Bride,
In all the Postures of her Face,
Which Nature gives in such a Case;   240
Distortions, Groanings, Strainings, Heavings;
'Twere better you had lickt her Leavings,
Than from Experience find too late
Your Goddess grown a filthy Mate.
Your Fancy then had always dwelt   245
On what you saw, and what you smelt;
Would still the same Ideas give ye,
As when you spy'd her on the Privy.
And, spight of *Chloe*'s Charms divine,
Your Heart had been as whole as mine.   250
    AUTHORITIES both old and recent
Direct that Women must be decent;
And, from the Spouse each Blemish hide
More than from all the World beside.
    UNJUSTLY all our Nymphs complain,   255
Their Empire holds so short a Reign;
Is after Marriage lost so soon,
It hardly holds the Honeymoon:
For, if they keep not what they caught,
It is entirely their own Fault.   260
They take Possession of the Crown,
And then throw all their Weapons down;
Though by the Politicians Scheme
Whoe'er arrives at Pow'r supreme,
Those Arts by which at first they gain it,   265
They still must practise to maintain it.
    WHAT various Ways our Females take,
To pass for Wits before a Rake!
And in the fruitless Search pursue
All other Methods but the true.   270
    SOME try to learn polite Behaviour,
By reading Books against their Saviour;
Some call it witty to reflect
On ev'ry natural Defect;
Some shew they never want explaining,   275
To comprehend a double Meaning.
But, sure a Tell-tale out of School
Is of all Wits the greatest Fool;
Whose rank Imagination fills,
Her Heart, and from her Lips distills;   280
You'd think she utter'd from behind,

Or at her Mouth was breaking Wind.
　WHY is a handsome Wife ador'd
By ev'ry Coxcomb, but her Lord?
From yonder Puppet-Man inquire,　　　　　　　285
Who wisely hides his Wood and Wire;
Shews *Sheba*'s Queen completely drest,
And *Solomon* in Royal Vest;
But, view them litter'd on the Floor,
Or strung on Pegs behind the Door;　　　　　290
Punch is exactly of a Piece
With *Lorraine*'s Duke, and Prince of *Greece*.
　A PRUDENT Builder should forecast
How long the Stuff is like to last;
And, carefully observe the Ground,　　　　　295
To build on some Foundation sound;
What House, when its Materials crumble,
Must not inevitably tumble?
What Edifice can long endure,
Rais'd on a Basis unsecure?　　　　　　　300
Rash Mortals, e'er you take a Wife,
Contrive your Pile to last for Life;
Since Beauty scarce endures a Day,
And Youth so swiftly glides away;
Why will you make yourself a Bubble　　　305
To build on Sand with Hay and Stubble?
　ON Sense and Wit your Passion found,
By Decency cemented round;
Let Prudence with Good Nature strive,
To keep Esteem and Love alive.　　　　　　310
Then come old Age whene'er it will,
Your Friendship shall continue still:
And thus a mutual gentle Fire,
Shall never but with Life expire.

The Lady's Dressing Room

Five Hours (and who can do it less in?)
By haughty *Celia* spent in Dressing;
The Goddess from her Chamber issues,
Arrayed in Lace, Brocades and Tissues.
Strephon, who found the Room was void,　　　5
And *Betty* otherwise employed;
Stole in, and took a strict Survey,
Of all the Litter as it lay;
Whereof, to make the Matter clear,
An Inventory follows here.　　　　　　　　　10

And first a dirty Smock appeared,
Beneath the Armpits well besmeared.
Strephon, the Rogue, displayed it wide,
And turned it round on every Side.
On such a Point few Words are best,   15
And *Strephon* bids us guess the rest;
But swears how damnably the Men lie,
In calling *Celia* sweet and cleanly.
Now listen while he next produces,
The various Combs for various Uses,   20
Filled up with Dirt so closely fixed,
No Brush could force a way betwixt.
A Paste of Composition rare,
Sweat, Dandruff, Powder, Lead, and Hair;
A Forehead Cloth with Oil upon't   25
To smooth the wrinkles on her Front;
Here Alum Flower to stop the Steams,
Exhaled from sour unsavoury Streams,
There Night-gloves made of Tripsy's Hide,
Bequeathed by Tripsy when she died,   30
With Puppy Water, Beauty's Help
Distilled from Tripsy's darling Whelp;
Here Gallipots and Vials placed,
Some filled with Washes, some with Paste,
Some with Pomatum, Paints and Slops,   35
And Ointments good for scabby Chops,
Hard by a filthy Basin stands,
Fouled with the Scouring of her Hands;
The Basin takes whatever comes
The Scrapings of her Teeth and Gums,   40
A nasty Compound of all Hues,
For here she spits, and here she spues.
But oh! it turned poor *Strephon*'s Bowels,
When he beheld and smelt the Towels,
Begummed, bemattered, and beslimed   45
With Dirt, and Sweat, and Ear-Wax grimed.
No Object *Strephon*'s Eye escapes,
here Petticoats in frowzy Heaps;
Nor be the Handkerchiefs forgot
All varnished o'er with Snuff and Snot.   50
The Stockings, why should I expose,
Stained with the Marks of stinking Toes;
Or greasy Coifs and Pinners reeking
Which *Celia* slept at least a Week in?
A Pair of Tweezers next he found   55
To pluck her Brows in Arches round,
Or Hairs that sink the Forehead low,
Or on her Chin like Bristles grow.

The Virtues we must not let pass,
Of *Celia's* magnifying Glass.   60
When frighted *Strephon* cast his Eye on't
It showed the Visage of a Giant.
A Glass that can to Sight disclose,
The smallest Worm in *Celia's* Nose,
And faithfully direct her Nail   65
To squeeze it out from Head to Tail;
For catch it nicely by the Head,
It must come out alive or dead.
    Why *Strephon* will you tell the rest?
And must you needs describe the Chest?   70
That careless Wench! no Creature warn her
To move it out from yonder Corner;
But leave it standing full in Sight
For you to exercise your Spite.
In vain, the Workman showed his Wit   75
With Rings and Hinges counterfeit
To make it seem in this Disguise,
A Cabinet to vulgar Eyes;
For *Strephon* ventured to look in,
Resolved to go through thick and thin;   80
He lifts the Lid, there needs no more,
He smelt it all the Time before.
As from within *Pandora's* Box,
When *Epimetheus* op'd the Locks,
A sudden universal Crew   85
Of human Evils upwards flew;
He still was comforted to find
That *Hope* at last remained behind;
So *Strephon* lifting up the Lid,
To view what in the Chest was hid.   90
The Vapours flew from out the Vent,
But *Strephon* cautious never meant
The Bottom of the Pan to grope,
And foul his Hands in Search of *Hope*.
O never may such vile Machine   95
Be once in *Celia's* Chamber seen!
O may she better learn to keep
'Those Secrets of the hoary deep!'[1]
    As Mutton Cutlets, Prime of Meat,
Which though with Art you salt and beat,   100
As laws of Cookery require,
And toast them at the clearest Fire;
If from adown the hopeful Chops
The Fat upon a Cinder drops,

---

[1]   Milton [*Paradise Lost* 2:891].

To stinking Smoke it turns the Flame   105
Poisoning the Flesh from whence it came;
And up exhales a greater Stench,
For which you curse the careless Wench;
So Things, which must not be expressed,
When plumped into the reeking chest;   110
Send up an excremental Smell
To taint the Parts from whence they fell.
The Petticoats and Gown perfume,
Which waft a Stink round every Room.
   Thus finishing his grand Survey,   115
Disgusted *Strephon* stole away
Repeating in his amorous Fits,
Oh! *Celia*, *Celia*, *Celia* shits!
   But Vengeance Goddess never sleeping
Soon punished *Strephon* for his Peeping;   120
His foul Imagination links
Each Dame he sees with all her Stinks:
And, if unsav'ry Odours fly,
Conceives a Lady standing by;
All Women his Description fits,   125
And both Ideas jump like Wits:
By vicious Fancy coupled fast,
And still appearing in Contrast.
I pity wretched *Strephon* blind
To all the Charms of Female Kind;   130
Should I the Queen of Love refuse,
Because she rose from stinking Ooze?
To him that looks behind the Scene,
Statira's but some pocky Quean.
When *Celia* in her Glory shows,   135
If *Strephon* would but stop his Nose
(Who now so impiously blasphemes
Her Ointments, Daubs, and Paints and Creams,
Her Washes, Slops, and every Clout,
With which he makes so foul a Rout),   140
He soon would learn to think like me,
And bless his ravished Sight to see
Such Order from Confusion sprung,
Such gaudy Tulips raised from Dung.

A Beautiful Young Nymph Going to Bed
Written for the Honour of the Fair Sex

Corinna, Pride of *Drury Lane*,
For whom no Shepherd sighs in vain;

Never did *Covent Garden* boast
So bright a battered, strolling Toast;
No drunken Rake to pick her up,   5
No Cellar where on Tick to sup;
Returning at the Midnight Hour;
Four Stories climbing to her Bow'r;
Then, seated on a three-legg'd Chair,
Takes off her artificial Hair: 10
Now, picking out a Crystal Eye,
She wipes it clean, and lays it by.
Her Eye-brows from a Mouse's Hide,
Stuck on with Art on either Side,
Pulls off with Care, and first displays 'em,   15
Then in a Playbook smoothly lays 'em.
Now dext'rously her Plumpers draws,
That serve to fill her hollow Jaws.
Untwists a Wire; and from her Gums
A Set of Teeth completely comes.   20
Pulls out the Rags contrived to prop
Her flabby Dugs, and down they drop.
Proceeding on, the lovely Goddess
Unlaces next her Steel-ribbed Bodice;
Which, by the Operator's Skill,   25
Press down the Lumps, the Hollows fill.
Up goes her Hand, and off she slips
The Bolsters that supply her Hips
With gentlest Touch, she next explores
Her Shankers, Issues, running Sores;   30
Effects of many a sad Disaster,
And then to each applies a Plaster.
But must, before she goes to Bed,
Rub off the Daubs of White and Red.
And smooth the Furrows in her Front,   35
With greasy Paper stuck upon't.
She takes a *Bolus* ere she sleeps;
And then between two Blankets creeps.
With Pains of Love tormented lies;
Or, if she chance to close her Eyes,   40
Of *Bridewell* and the *Compter* dreams,
And feels the Lash, and faintly screams.
Or, by a faithless Bully drawn,
At some Hedge-Tavern lies in Pawn.
Or to Jamaica seems transported,   45
Alone, and by no Planter courted;
Or, near *Fleet-Ditch*'s oozy Brinks,
Surrounded with a Hundred Stinks,
Belated, seems on Watch to lie,
And snap some Cully passing by;   50

Or, struck with Fear, her Fancy runs
On Watchmen, Constables and Duns,
From whom she meets with frequent Rubs;
But, never from religious Clubs;
Whose Favour she is sure to find,   55
Because she pays them all in Kind.
    Corinna wakes. A dreadful Sight!
Behold the Ruins of the Night!
A wicked Rat her Plaister stole,
Half eat, and dragged it to his Hole.   60
The Crystal Eye, alas, was missed;
And Puss had on her plumpers pissed;
A Pigeon picked her Issue-peas;
And *Shock* her *Tresses* filled with fleas.
    The Nymph, though in this mangled Plight,   65
Must every Morn her Limbs unite;
But, how shall I describe her Arts
To recollect her scattered Parts?
Or show the Anguish, Toil, and Pain,
Of gathering up herself again?   70
The bashful Muse will never bear
In such a Scene to interfere.
Corinna in the Morning dizened,
Who sees will spew; who smells be poisoned.

Cassinus and *Peter*. A Tragical Elegy

Two College Sophs of *Cambridge* Growth,
Both special Wits, and Lovers both,
Conferring as they us'd to meet,
On Love and Books in Rapture sweet;
(Muse, find me Names to fix my Metre,   5
Cassinus this, and t' other *Peter*)
Friend *Peter* to *Cassinus* goes,
To chat a while, and warm his Nose:
But, such a Sight was never seen,
The Lad lay swallow'd up in Spleen;   10
He seem'd as just crept out of Bed;
One greasy Stocking round his Head,
The t' other he sat down to darn
With Threads of diff'rent colour'd Yarn.
His Breeches torn exposing wide   15
A ragged Shirt, and tawny Hyde.
Scorcht were his Shins, his Legs were bare,
But, well embrown'd with Dirt and Hair.
A Rug was o'er his Shoulders thrown;
A Rug; for Night-gown he had none.   20

His Jordan stood in Manner fitting
Between his Legs, to spew or spit in.
His antient Pipe in Sable dy'd,
And half unsmoakt, lay by his Side,
   HIM thus accoutred *Peter* found,   25
With Eyes in Smoak and Weeping drown'd:
The Leavings of his last Night's Pot
On Embers plac'd, to drink it hot.
   WHY, *Cassy*, thou wilt doze thy Pate:
What makes thee lie a-bed so late?   30
The Finch, the Linnet and the Thrush,
Their Mattins chant in ev'ry Bush:
And, I have heard thee oft salute
Aurora with thy early Flute.
Heaven send thou hast not got the Hypps.   35
How? Not a Word come from thy lips?
   THEN gave him some familiar Thumps,
A College Joke to cure the Dumps.
   THE Swain at last, with Grief opprest,
Cry'd, *Cælia!* thrice, and sigh'd the rest.   40
   DEAR *Cassy*, though to ask I dread,
Yet, ask I must. Is *Cælia* dead?
   How happy I, were that the worst?
But I was fated to be curs'd.
   COME, tell us, has she play'd the Whore?   45
   OH *Peter*, wou'd it were no more!
   WHY, Plague confound her sandy Locks:
Say, has the small or greater Pox
Sunk down her Nose, or seam'd her Face?
Be easy, 'tis a common Case.   50
   OH *Peter!* Beauty's but a Varnish,
Which Time and Accidents will tarnish:
But, *Cælia* has contriv'd to blast
Those Beauties that might ever last.
Nor can Imagination guess,   55
Nor Eloquence Divine express,
How that ungrateful charming Maid,
My purest Passion has betray'd.
Conceive the most invenom'd Dart,
To pierce an injur'd Lover's Heart.   60
   WHY, hang her, though she seem'd so coy,
I know she loves the Barber's Boy.
   FRIEND *Peter*, this I could excuse;
For, ev'ry Nymph has Leave to chuse;
Nor, have I Reason to complain: 65
She loves a more deserving Swain.
But, oh! how ill hast thou divin'd
A Crime that shocks all human Kind;

A Deed unknown to Female Race,
At which the Sun should hide his Face.   70
Advice in vain you would apply—
Then, leave me to despair and dye.
Yet, kind *Arcadians*, on my Urn
These Elegies and Sonnets burn,
And on the Marble grave these Rhimes,   75
A Monument to after-Times:
'Here *Cassy* lies, by *Cælia* slain,
And dying, never told his Pain.'
    VAIN empty World farewel. But hark,
The loud *Cerberian* triple Bark.   80
And there——behold *Alecto* stand,
A Whip of Scorpions in her Hand.
Lo, *Charon* from his leaky Wherry,
Beck'ning to waft me o'er the Ferry.
I come, I come,—*Medusa*, see,   85
Her Serpents hiss direct at me.
Begone; unhand me, hellish Fry;
Avaunt—ye cannot say 'twas I.
    DEAR *Cassy*, thou must purge and bleed;
I fear thou wilt be mad indeed.   90
But now, by Friendship's sacred Laws,
I here conjure thee, tell the Cause;
And *Cælia*'s horrid Fact relate;
Thy Friend would gladly share thy Fate.
    To force it out my Heart must rend;   95
Yet, when conjur'd by such a Friend—
Think, *Peter*, how my Soul is rack'd.
These Eyes, these Eyes beheld the Fact.
Now, bend thine Ear; since out it must:
But, when thou seest me laid in Dust,   100
The Secret thou shalt ne'er impart;
Not to the Nymph that keeps thy Heart;
(How would her Virgin Soul bemoan
A Crime to all her Sex unknown!)
Nor whisper to the tattling Reeds,   105
The blackest of all Female Deeds.
Nor blab it on the lonely Rocks,
Where Echo sits, and list'ning mocks.
Nor let the Zephyr's treach'rous Gale
Through *Cambridge* waft the direful Tale.   110
Nor to the chattering feather'd Race,
Discover *Cælia*'s foul Disgrace.
But, if you fail, my Spectre dread
Attending nightly round your Bed;
And yet, I dare confide in you;   115

So, take my Secret, and adieu.
　　NOR wonder how I lost my Wits;
Oh! *Cælia, Cælia Cælia* shits.

Verses on the Death of Dr *Swift*, D.S.P.D.

Occasioned by reading a maxim in Rochefoucault

Dans l'adversité de nos meilleurs amis nous trouvons quelque chose, qui
ne nous deplaist pas.
In the Adversity of our best Friends, we find something that doth not
displease us.

　　As *Rochefoucault* his Maxims drew
　　From Nature, I believe 'em true:
　　They argue no corrupted Mind
　　In him; the Fault is in Mankind.
　　　THIS Maxim more than all the rest　　　　　　　5
　　Is thought too base for human Breast;
　　'In all Distresses of our Friends
　　We first consult our private Ends,
　　While Nature kindly bent to ease us,
　　Points out some Circumstance to please us.'　　　10
　　　IF this perhaps your Patience move
　　Let Reason and Experience prove.
　　　WE all behold with envious Eyes,
　　Our *Equal* rais'd above our *Size*;
　　Who wou'd not at a crowded Show,　　　　　　　15
　　Stand high himself, keep others low?
　　I love my Friend as well as you,
　　But would not have him stop my View;
　　Then let him have the higher Post;
　　I ask but for an Inch at most.　　　　　　　　　20
　　　IF in a Battle you should find,
　　One, whom you love of all Mankind,
　　Had some heroick Action done,
　　A Champion kill'd, or Trophy won;
　　Rather than thus be over-topt,　　　　　　　　25
　　Would you not wish his Lawrels cropt?
　　　DEAR honest *Ned* is in the Gout,
　　Lies rackt with Pain, and you without:
　　How patiently you hear him groan!
　　How glad the Case is not your own!　　　　　　30
　　　WHAT Poet would not grieve to see,
　　His Brethren write as well as he?
　　But rather than they should excel,
　　He'd wish his Rivals all in Hell.

HER End when Emulation Hisses,   35
She turns to Envy, Stings and Hisses:
The strongest Friendship yields to Pride,
Unless the Odds be on our Side.
   VAIN human Kind! Fantastick Race!
Thy various Follies, who can trace?   40
Self-love, Ambition, Envy, Pride,
Their Empire in our Hearts divide:
Give others Riches, Power, and Station,
'Tis all on me an Usurpation.
I have no Title to aspire;   45
Yet, when you sink, I seem the higher.
In POPE, I cannot read a Line,
But with a Sigh, I wish it mine:
When he can in one Couplet fix
More Sense than I can do in Six: 50
It gives me such a jealous Fit,
I cry, Pox take him, and his Wit.
   WHY must I be outdone by GAY,
In my own hum'rous biting Way?
   ARBUTHNOT is no more my Friend,   55
Who dares to Irony pretend;
Which I was born to introduce,
Refin'd it first, and shew'd its Use.
   ST. JOHN, as well as PULTNEY knows,
That I had some repute for Prose;   60
And till they drove me out of Date,
Could maul a Minister of State:
If they have mortify'd my Pride,
And made me throw my Pen aside;
If with such Talents Heav'n hath blest 'em   65
Have I not Reason to detest 'em?
   To all my Foes, dear Fortune, send
Thy Gifts, but never to my Friend:
I tamely can endure the first,
But, this with Envy makes me burst.   70
   THUS much may serve by way of Proem,
Proceed we therefore to our Poem.
   THE Time is not remote, when I
Must by the Course of Nature dye:
When I foresee my special Friends,   75
Will try to find their private Ends:
Tho' it is hardly understood,
Which way my Death can do them good;
Yet, thus methinks, I hear 'em speak:
See, how the Dean begins to break: 80
Poor Gentleman, he droops apace,
You plainly find it in his Face:

That old Vertigo in his Head,
Will never leave him, till he's dead:
Besides, his Memory decays,   85
He recollects not what he says;
He cannot call his Friends to Mind;
Forgets the Place where last he din'd:
Plyes you with Stories o'er and o'er,
He told them fifty Times before.   90
How does he fancy we can sit,
To hear his out-of-fashion'd Wit?
But he takes up with younger Fokes,
Who for his Wine will bear his Jokes:
Faith, he must make his Stories shorter,   95
Or change his Comrades once a Quarter:
In half the Time, he talks them round;
There must another Sett be found.

   FOR Poetry, he's past his Prime,
He takes an Hour to find a Rhime: 100
His Fire is out, his Wit decay'd,
His Fancy sunk, his Muse a Jade.
I'd have him throw away his Pen;
But there's no talking to some Men.

   AND, then their Tenderness appears,   105
By adding largely to my Years:
'He's older than he would be reckon'd,
And well remembers *Charles* the Second.

   HE hardly drinks a Pint of Wine;
And that, I doubt, is no good Sign.   110
His Stomach too begins to fail:
Last Year we thought him strong and hale;
But now, he's quite another Thing;
I wish he may hold out till Spring.'

   THEN hug themselves, and reason thus;   115
'It is not yet so bad with us.'

   IN such a Case they talk in Tropes,
And, by their Fears express their Hopes:
Some great Misfortune to portend,
No Enemy can match a Friend;   120
With all the Kindness they profess,
The Merit of a lucky Guess,
(When daily Howd'y's come of Course,
And Servants answer; *Worse and Worse*)
Would please 'em better than to tell,   125
That, GOD be prais'd, the Dean is well.
Then he who prophecy'd the best,
Approves his Foresight to the rest:
'You know, I always fear'd the worst,
And often told you so at first:'   130

He'd rather chuse that I should dye,
Than his Prediction prove a Lye.
Not one foretels I shall recover;
But, all agree, to give me over.

YET should some Neighbour feel a Pain,   135
Just in the Parts, where I complain;
How many a Message would he send?
What hearty Prayers that I should mend?
Enquire what Regimen I kept;
What gave me Ease, and how I slept?   140
And more lament, when I was dead,
Than all the Sniv'llers round my Bed.

MY good Companions, never fear,
For though you may mistake a Year;
Though your Prognosticks run too fast,   145
They must be verify'd at last.

'BEHOLD the fatal Day arrive!
How is the Dean? He's just alive.
Now the departing Prayer is read:
He hardly breathes. The Dean is dead.   150
Before the Passing-Bell begun,
The News thro' half the Town has run.
O, may we all for Death prepare!
What has he left? And who's his Heir?
I know no more than what the News is,   155
'Tis all bequeath'd to publick Uses.
To publick Use! A perfect Whim!
What had the Publick done for him!
Meer Envy, Avarice, and Pride!
He gave it all:—But first he dy'd.   160
And had the Dean, in all the Nation,
No worthy Friend, no poor Relation?
So ready to do Strangers good,
Forgetting his own Flesh and Blood?'

NOW Grub-Street Wits are all employ'd;   165
With Elegies, the Town is cloy'd:
Some Paragraph in ev'ry Paper,
To *curse* the *Dean*, or *bless* the *Drapier*.

THE Doctors tender of their Fame,
Wisely on me lay all the Blame: 170
'We must confess his Case was nice;
But he would never take Advice:
Had he been rul'd, for ought appears,
He might have liv'd these Twenty Years:
For when we open'd him we found,   175
That all his vital Parts were sound.'

FROM *Dublin* soon to *London* spread,
Tis told at Court, the Dean is dead.

KIND Lady *Suffolk* in the Spleen,
Runs laughing up to tell the Queen.   180
The Queen, so Gracious, Mild, and Good,
Cries, 'Is he gone? 'Tis time he should.
He's dead you say; why let him rot;
I'm glad the Medals were forgot.
I promis'd them, I own; but when?   185
I only was the Princess then;
But now as Consort of the King,
You know 'tis quite a different Thing.'
    Now, *Chartres* at Sir *Robert*'s Levee,
Tells, with a Sneer, the Tidings heavy: 190
'Why, is he dead without his Shoes?
(Cries *Bob*) 'I'm Sorry for the News;
Oh, were the Wretch but living still,
And in his Place my good Friend *Will*;
Or, had a Mitre on his Head   195
Provided *Bolingbroke* were dead.'
    Now *Curl* his Shop from Rubbish drains;
Three genuine Tomes of *Swift*'s Remains.
And then to make them pass the glibber,
Revis'd by *Tibbalds, Moore, and Cibber.*   200
He'll treat me as he does my Betters.
Publish my Will, my Life, my Letters.
Revive the Libels born to dye;
Which POPE must bear, as well as I.
    Here shift the Scene, to represent   205
How those I love, my Death lament.
Poor POPE will grieve a Month; and GAY
A Week; and ARBUTHNOTT a Day.
    ST. JOHN himself will scarce forbear,
To bite his Pen, and drop a Tear.   210
The rest will give a Shrug and cry,
I'm sorry; but we all must dye.
Indifference clad in Wisdom's Guise,
All Fortitude of Mind supplies:
For how can stony Bowels melt,   215
In those who never Pity felt;
When *We* are lash'd, *They* kiss the Rod;
Resigning to the Will of God.
    THE Fools, my Juniors by a Year,
Are tortur'd with Suspence and Fear.   220
Who wisely thought my Age a Screen,
When Death approach'd, to stand between:
The Screen remov'd, their Hearts are trembling,
They mourn for me without dissembling.
    MY female Friends, whose tender Hearts   225
Have better learn'd to act their Parts.

Receive the News in *doleful Dumps*,
'The Dean is dead, (*and what is Trumps?*)
Then Lord have Mercy on his Soul.
(Ladies I'll venture for the *Vole*.)   230
Six Deans they say must bear the Pall.
(I wish I knew what *King* to call.)
Madam, your Husband will attend
The Funeral of so good a Friend.
No Madam, 'tis a shocking Sight,   235
And he's engag'd Tomorrow Night!
My Lady *Club* wou'd take it ill,
If he shou'd fail her at *Quadrill*.
He lov'd the Dean. (*I lead a Heart*.)
But dearest Friends, they say, must part.   240
His Time was come, he ran his Race;
We hope he's in a better Place.'
   WHY do we grieve that Friends should dye?
No Loss more easy to supply.
One Year is past; a different Scene;   245
No further mention of the Dean;
Who now, alas, no more is mist,
Than if he never did exist.
Where's now this Fav'rite of *Apollo*?
Departed; *and his Works must follow*:   250
Must undergo the common Fate;
His Kind of Wit is out of Date.
Some Country Squire to *Lintot* goes,
Enquires for SWIFT in Verse and Prose:
Says *Lintot*, 'I have heard the Name: 255
He dy'd a Year ago.' The same.
He searcheth all his Shop in vain;
'Sir you may find them in *Duck-lane*:
I sent them with a Load of Books,
Last *Monday* to the Pastry-cooks.   260
To fancy they cou'd live a Year!
I find you're but a Stranger here.
The Dean was famous in his Time;
And had a Kind of Knack at Rhyme:
His way of Writing now is past;   265
The Town hath got a better Taste:
I keep no antiquated Stuff;
But, spick and span I have enough.
Pray, do but give me leave to shew 'em;
Here's *Colley Cibber*'s Birth-day Poem.   270
This Ode you never yet have seen,
By *Stephen Duck*, upon the Queen.
Then, here's a Letter finely penn'd
Against the *Craftsman* and his Friend;

It clearly shews that all Reflection   275
On Ministers, is disaffection.
Next, here's Sir *Robert*'s Vindication,
And Mr. *Henly*'s last Oration:
The Hawkers have not got 'em yet,
Your Honour please to buy a Set?   280
   HERE's *Wolston*'s Tracts, the twelfth Edition;
'Tis read by ev'ry Politician:
The Country Members, when in Town,
To all their Boroughs send them down:
You never met a Thing so smart;   285
The Courtiers have them all by Heart:
Those Maids of Honour (who can read)
Are taught to use them for their Creed.
The Rev'rend Author's good Intention,
Hath been rewarded with a Pension: 290
He doth an Honour to his Gown,
By bravely running *Priest-craft* down:
He shews, as sure as GOD's in *Gloc'ster*,
That *Jesus* was a Grand Impostor:
That all his Miracles were Cheats,   295
Perform'd as Juglers do their Feats:
The Church had never such a Writer:
A Shame, he hath not got a Mitre!'
   SUPPOSE me dead; and then suppose
A Club assembled at the *Rose*;   300
Where from Discourse of this and that,
I grow the Subject of their Chat:
And, while they toss my Name about,
With Favour some, and some without;
One quite indiff'rent in the Cause,   305
My Character impartial draws:
   'THE Dean, if we believe Report,
Was never ill receiv'd at Court:
As for his Works in Verse and Prose,
I own my self no Judge of those: 310
Nor, can I tell what Criticks thought 'em;
But, this I know, all People bought 'em;
As with a moral View design'd
To cure the Vices of Mankind:
His Vein, ironically grave,   315
Expos'd the Fool, and lash'd the Knave:
To steal a Hint was never known,
But what he writ was all his own.
   HE never thought an Honour done him,
Because a Duke was proud to own him: 320
Would rather slip aside, and chuse
To talk with Wits in dirty Shoes:

Despis'd the Fools with Stars and Garters,
So often seen caressing *Chartres:*
He never courted Men in Station,   325
Nor Persons had in Admiration;
Of no Man's Greatness was afraid,
Because he sought for no Man's Aid.
Though trusted long in great Affairs,
He gave himself no haughty Airs: 330
Without regarding private Ends,
Spent all his Credit for his Friends:
And only chose the Wise and Good;
No Flatt'rers; no Allies in Blood;
But succour'd Virtue in Distress,   335
And seldom fail'd of good Success;
As Numbers in their Hearts must own,
Who, but for him, had been unknown.
    WITH Princes kept a due Decorum,
But never stood in Awe before 'em: 340
He follow'd *David*'s Lesson just,
In Princes never put thy Trust.
And, would you make him truly sower;
Provoke him with *a slave in Power:*
The *Irish* Senate, if you nam'd,   345
With what Impatience he declaim'd!
Fair LIBERTY was all his Cry;
For her he stood prepar'd to die;
For her he boldly stood alone;
For her he oft expos'd his own.   350
Two Kingdoms, just as Faction led,
Had set a Price upon his Head;
But, not a Traytor cou'd be found,
To sell him for Six Hundred Pound.
    HAD he but spar'd his Tongue and Pen,   355
He might have rose like other Men:
But, Power was never in his Thought;
And, Wealth he valu'd not a Groat:
Ingratitude he often found,
And pity'd those who meant the Wound: 360
But, kept the Tenor of his Mind,
To merit well of human Kind:
Nor made a Sacrifice of those
Who still were true, to please his Foes.
He labour'd many a fruitless Hour   365
To reconcile his Friends in Power;
Saw Mischief by a Faction brewing,
While they pursu'd each others Ruin.
But, finding vain was all his Care,
He left the Court in meer Despair.   370

AND, oh! how short are human Schemes!
Here ended all our golden Dreams.
What ST. JOHN's Skill in State Affairs,
What ORMOND's *Valour*, OXFORD's Cares,
To save their sinking Country lent,   375
Was all destroy'd by one Event.
Too soon that precious Life was ended,
On which alone, our Weal depended.
When up a dangerous Faction starts,
With Wrath and Vengeance in their Hearts: 380
By solemn League and Cov'nant bound,
To ruin, slaughter, and confound;
To turn Religion to a Fable,
And make the Government a *Babel:*
Pervert the Law, disgrace the Gown,   385
Corrupt the Senate, rob the Crown;
To sacrifice old *England*'s Glory,
And make her infamous in Story.
When such a Tempest shook the Land,
How could unguarded Virtue stand?   390
   WITH Horror, Grief, Despair the Dean
Beheld the dire destructive Scene:
His Friends in Exile, or the Tower,
Himself within the Frown of Power;
Pursu'd by base envenom'd Pens,   395
Far to the Land of Slaves and Fens;
A servile Race in Folly nurs'd,
Who truckle most, when treated worst.
   BY Innocence and Resolution,
He bore continual Persecution;   400
While Numbers to Preferment rose;
Whose Merits were, to be his Foes.
When, *ev'n his own familiar Friends*
Intent upon their private Ends;
Like Renegadoes now he feels,   405
Against him lifting up their Heels.
   'THE Dean did by his Pen defeat
An infamous destructive Cheat.
Taught Fools their Int'rest how to know;
And gave them Arms to ward the Blow.   410
Envy hath own'd it was his doing,
To save that helpless Land from Ruin,
While they who at the Steerage stood,
And reapt the Profit, sought his Blood.
   TO save them from their evil Fate,   415
In him was held a Crime of State.
A wicked Monster on the Bench,
Whose Fury Blood could never quench;

As vile and profligate a Villain,
As modern *Scroggs*, or old *Tressilian*;   420
Who long all Justice had discarded,
Nor fear'd he GOD, nor Man regarded;
Vow'd on the Dean his Rage to vent,
And make him of his Zeal repent;
But Heav'n his Innocence defends,   425
The grateful People stand his Friends:
Not Strains of Law, nor Judges Frown,
Nor Topicks brought to please the Crown,
Nor Witness hir'd, nor Jury pick'd,
Prevail to bring him in convict.   430
  IN Exile with a steady Heart,
He spent his Life's declining Part;
Where, Folly, Pride, and Faction sway,
Remote from ST. JOHN, POPE, and GAY.
  HIS Friendship there to few confin'd,   435
Were always of the midling Kind:
No Fools of Rank, a mungril Breed,
Who fain would pass for Lords indeed:
Where Titles give no Right or Power,
And Peerage is a wither'd Flower,   440
He would have held it a Disgrace,
If such a Wretch had known his Face.
On Rural Squires, that Kingdom's Bane,
He vented oft his Wrath in vain:
Biennial Squires, to Market brought;   445
Who sell their Souls and Votes for Naught;
The Nation stript go joyful back,
To rob the Church, their Tenants rack,
Go Snacks with Thieves and Rapparees,
And, keep the Peace, to pick up Fees: 450
In every Jobb to have a Share,
A Jayl or Barrack to repair;
And turn the Tax for publick Roads
Commodious to their own Abodes.
  PERHAPS I may allow, the Dean   455
Had too much Satyr in his Vein;
And seem'd determin'd not to starve it,
Because no Age could more deserve it.
Yet, Malice never was his Aim;
He lash'd the Vice but spar'd the Name.   460
No Individual could resent,
Where Thousands equally were meant.
His Satyr points at no Defect,
But what all Mortals may correct;
For he abhorr'd that senseless Tribe,   465
Who call it Humour when they jibe:

He spar'd a Hump or crooked Nose,
Whose Owners set not up for Beaux.
True genuine Dulness mov'd his Pity,
Unless it offer'd to be witty.   470
Those, who their Ignorance confess'd,
He ne'er offended with a Jest;
But laugh'd to hear an Idiot quote,
A Verse from *Horace*, learn'd by Rote.
    HE knew an hundred pleasant Stories,   475
'With all the Turns of *Whigs* and *Tories:*
Was chearful to his dying Day,
And Friends would let him have his Way.
    HE gave the little Wealth he had,
To build a House for Fools and Mad: 480
And shew'd by one satyric Touch,
No Nation wanted it so much:
That Kingdom he hath left his Debtor,
I wish it soon may have a Better.'

Alexander Pope
(1688–1744)

Epistle to Miss Blount, with the Works of Voiture

IN these gay thoughts the Loves and Graces shine,
And all the writer lives in ev'ry line;
His easy art may happy nature seem,
Trifles themselves are elegant in him.
Sure to charm all was his peculiar fate, 5
Who without flattery pleased the fair and great;
Still with esteem no less conversed than read;
With wit well-natured, and with books well-bred;
His heart, his mistress and his friend did share,
His time, the Muse, the witty and the fair. 10
Thus wisely careless, innocently gay,
Cheerful he play'd the trifle, Life, away;
Till fate scarce felt his gentle breath suppressed,
As smiling infants sport themselves to rest.
Even rival wits did Voiture's death deplore, 15
And the gay mourn'd who never mourn'd before;
The truest hearts for Voiture heaved with sighs,
Voiture was wept by all the brightest eyes:
The Smiles and Loves had died in Voiture's death,
But that for ever in his lines they breathe. 20
   Let the strict life of graver mortals be
A long, exact, and serious comedy;
In ev'ry scene some moral let it teach,
And, if it can, at once both please and preach.
Let mine, an innocent gay farce appear, 25
And more diverting still than regular,
Have humour, wit, a native ease and grace,
Though not too strictly bound to time and place:
Critics in wit, or life, are hard to please,
Few write to those, and none can live to these. 30
   Too much your sex is by their forms confined,
Severe to all, but most to womankind;
Custom, grown blind with age, must be your guide;
Your pleasure is a vice, but not your pride;
By nature yielding, stubborn but for fame; 35

Made slaves by honour, and made fools by shame.
Marriage may all those petty tyrants chase,
But sets up one, a greater, in their place:
Well might you wish for change by those accursed,
But the last tyrant ever proves the worst.   40
Still in constraint your suff'ring sex remains,
Or bound in formal or in real chains:
Whole years neglected, for some months adored,
The fawning servant turns a haughty lord.
Ah quit not the free innocence of life,   45
For the dull glory of a virtuous wife;
Nor let false shows nor empty titles please:
Aim not at joy, but rest content with ease.
    The gods, to curse Pamela with her prayers,
Gave the gilt coach and dappled Flanders mares,   50
The shining robes, rich jewels, beds of state,
And, to complete her bliss, a fool for mate.
She glares in balls, front boxes, and the Ring,
A vain, unquiet, glitt'ring, wretched thing!
Pride, pomp, and state but reach her outward part;   55
She sighs, and is no duchess at her heart.
    But Madam, if the Fates withstand, and you
Are destined Hymen's willing victim too;
Trust not too much your now resistless charms,
Those, age or sickness soon or late disarms: 60
Good humour only teaches charms to last,
Still makes new conquests, and maintains the past:
Love, raised on beauty, will like that decay,
Our hearts may bear its slender chain a day;
As flowery bands in wantonness are worn,   65
A morning's pleasure, and at evening torn;
This binds in ties more easy, yet more strong,
The willing heart, and only holds it long.
    Thus Voiture's early care still shone the same,
And Monthausier was only changed in name;   70
By this, ev'n now they live, ev'n now they charm,
Their wit still sparkling, and their flames still warm.
    Now crown'd with myrtle, on th' Elysian coast,
Amid those lovers, joys his gentle ghost:
Pleased, while with smiles his happy lines you view,   75
And finds a fairer Rambouillet in you.
The brightest eyes in France inspired his Muse;
The brightest eyes of Britain now peruse;
And dead, as living, 'tis our author's pride
Still to charm those who charm the world beside.   80

The Rape of the Lock

DEDICATION TO MRS. ARABELLA FERMOR

MADAM,—It will be in vain to deny that I have some regard for this piece, since I dedicate it to you. Yet you may bear me witness, it was intended only to divert a few young ladies, who have good sense and good humour enough to laugh not only at their sex's little unguarded follies, but at their own. But as it was communicated with the air of a secret, it soon found its way into the world. An imperfect copy having been offered to a bookseller, you had the good-nature for my sake to consent to the publication of one more correct: this I was forced to before I had executed half my design, for the machinery was entirely wanting to complete it.

The machinery, Madam, is a term invented by the critics to signify that part which the Deities, Angels, or Dæmons are made to act in a Poem: for the ancient Poets are in one respect like many modern ladies: let an action be never so trivial in itself, they always make it appear of the utmost importance. These machines I determined to raise on a very new and odd foundation, the Rosicrucian doctrine of Spirits.

I know how disagreeable it is to make use of hard words before a lady; but 'tis so much the concern of a Poet to have his works understood, and particularly by your sex, that you must give me leave to explain two or three difficult terms.

The Rosicrucians are a people I must bring you acquainted with. The best account I know of them is in a French book called *Le Comte de Gabalis*, which, both in its title and size, is so like a novel that many of the fair sex have read it for one by mistake. According to these gentlemen, the four elements are inhabited by Spirits which they call Sylphs, Gnomes, Nymphs and Salamanders. The Gnomes, or Dæmons of Earth, delight in mischief; but the Sylphs, whose habitation is in the air, are the best-conditioned creatures imaginable. For they say any mortals may enjoy the most intimate familiarities with these gentle Spirits, upon a condition very easy to all true adepts, an inviolate preservation of chastity.

As to the following Cantos, all the passages of them are as fabulous as the vision at the beginning, or the transformation at the end (except the loss of your hair, which I always mention with reverence). The human persons are as fictitious as the airy ones; and the character of Belinda, as it is now managed, resembles you in nothing but in beauty.

If this Poem had as many graces as there are in your person, or in your mind, yet I could never hope it should pass through the world half so uncensured as you have done. But let its fortune be what it will, mine is happy enough, to have given me this occasion of assuring you that I am, with the truest esteem, Madam, your most obedient, humble Servant,

A. POPE.

Nolueram, Belinda, tuos violare capillos;
Sed juvat, hoc precibus me tribuisse tuis.—MART.

Canto I

What dire offence from amorous causes springs,
What mighty contests rise from trivial things,
I sing—This verse to CARYLL, Muse! is due:
This, even Belinda may vouchsafe to view;
Slight is the subject, but not so the praise,   5
If she inspire, and he approve my lays.
   Say what strange motive, goddess! could compel
A well-bred lord to assault a gentle belle?
O say what stranger cause, yet unexplored,
Could make a gentle belle reject a lord?   10
In tasks so bold, can little men engage,
And in soft bosoms dwells such mighty rage?
   Sol through white curtains shot a tim'rous ray,
And oped those eyes that must eclipse the day:
Now lap-dogs give themselves the rousing shake,   15
And sleepless lovers, just at twelve awake:
Thrice rung the bell, the slipper knock'd the ground,
And the press'd watch return'd a silver sound.
Belinda still her downy pillow press'd,
Her guardian sylph prolong'd the balmy rest: 20
'Twas he had summon'd to her silent bed
The morning-dream that hover'd o'er her head?
A youth more glittering than a birth-night beau,
(That ev'n in slumber caused her cheek to glow)
Seem'd to her ear his winning lips to lay,   25
And thus in whispers said, or seem'd to say:
   'Fairest of mortals, thou distinguish'd care
Of thousand bright inhabitants of air!
If e'er one vision touch'd thy infant thought,
Of all the nurse and all the priest have taught;   30
Of airy elves by moonlight shadows seen,
The silver token, and the circled green,
Or virgins visited by angel powers,
With golden crowns and wreaths of heavenly flowers;
Hear and believe! thy own importance know,   35
Nor bound thy narrow views to things below.
Some secret truths, from learned pride conceal'd,
To maids alone and children are reveal'd:
What though no credit doubting wits may give?
The fair and innocent shall still believe.   40
Know, then, unnumbered spirits round thee fly,
The light militia of the lower sky:
These, though unseen, are ever on the wing,
Hang o'er the box, and hover round the ring.
Think what an equipage thou hast in air,   45

And view with scorn two pages and a chair.
As now your own, our beings were of old,
And once inclosed in woman's beauteous mould;
Thence, by a soft transition, we repair
From earthly vehicles to these of air.   50
Think not, when woman's transient breath is fled,
That all her vanities at once are dead;
Succeeding vanities she still regards,
And though she plays no more, o'erlooks the cards.
Her joy in gilden chariots, when alive,   55
And love of ombre, after death survive.
For when the fair in all their pride expire,
To their first elements their souls retire:
The sprites of fiery termagants in flame
Mount up, and take a Salamander's name.   60
Soft yielding minds to water glide away,
And sip, with nymphs, their elemental tea.
The graver prude sinks downward to a gnome,
In search of mischief still on earth to roam.
The light coquettes in sylphs aloft repair,   65
And sport and flutter in the fields of air.
   'Know further yet; whoever fair and chaste
Rejects mankind, is by some sylph embraced:
For spirits, freed from mortal laws, with ease
Assume what sexes and what shapes they please.   70
What guards the purity of melting maids,
In courtly balls, and midnight masquerades,
Safe from the treach'rous friend, the daring spark,
The glance by day, the whisper in the dark,
When kind occasion prompts their warm desires,   75
When music softens, and when dancing fires?
'Tis but their sylph, the wise celestials know,
Though honour is the word with men below.
   'Some nymphs there are, too conscious of their face,
For life predestined to the gnomes embrace.   80
These swell their prospects and exalt their pride,
When offers are disdain'd and love denied:
Then gay ideas crowd the vacant brain,
While peers, and dukes, and all their sweeping train,
And garters, stars, and coronets appear,   85
And in soft sounds, "Your Grace" salutes their ear.
'Tis these that early taint the female soul,
Instruct the eyes of young coquettes to roll,
Teach infant cheeks a bidden blush to know,
And little hearts to flutter at a beau.   90
   'Oft when the world imagine women stray,
The sylphs through mystic mazes guide their way,
Through all the giddy circle they pursue,

And old impertinence expel by new.
What tender maid but must a victim fall   95
To one man's treat, but for another's ball?
When Florio speaks, what virgin could withstand,
If gentle Damon did not squeeze her hand?
With varying vanities, from ev'ry part,
They shift the moving toyshop of their heart;   100
Where wigs with wigs, with sword-knots sword-knots strive,
Beaux banish beaux, and coaches coaches drive.
This erring mortals levity may call,
Oh, blind to truth! the sylphs contrive it all.
    'Of these am I, who thy protection claim,   105
A watchful sprite, and Ariel is my name.
Late, as I ranged the crystal wilds of air,
In the clear mirror of thy ruling star
I saw, alas! some dread event impend,
Ere to the main this morning sun descend;   110
But heaven reveals not what, or how, or where:
Warn'd by the sylph, oh, pious maid, beware!
This to disclose is all thy guardian can:
Beware of all, but most beware of man!'
    He said; when Shock, who thought she slept too long,   115
Leap'd up, and waked his mistress with his tongue.
'Twas then, Belinda, if report say true,
Thy eyes first open'd on a billet-doux;
Wounds, charms, and ardours, were no sooner read,
But all the vision vanish'd from thy head.   120
    And now, unveil'd, the toilet stands display'd,
Each silver vase in mystic order laid.
First, robed in white, the nymph intent adores,
With head uncover'd, the cosmetic powers.
A heav'nly image in the glass appears,   125
To that she bends, to that her eye she rears;
Th' inferior priestess, at her altar's side,
Trembling, begins the sacred rites of pride.
Unnumber'd treasures ope at once, and here
The various offerings of the world appear;   130
From each she nicely culls with curious toil,
And decks the goddess with the glitt'ring spoil.
This casket India's glowing gems unlocks,
And all Arabia breathes from yonder box.
The tortoise here and elephant unite,   135
Transform'd to combs, the speckled and the white.
Here files of pins extend their shining rows,
Puffs, powders, patches, Bibles, billet-doux.
Now awful beauty puts on all its arms;
The fair each moment rises in her charms,   140
Repairs her smiles, awakens every grace,

And calls forth all the wonders of her face:
Sees by degrees a purer blush arise,
And keener lightnings quicken in her eyes.
The busy sylphs surround their darling care,   145
These set the head, and those divide the hair,
Some fold the sleeve, while others plait the gown:
And Betty's praised for labours not her own.

Canto II

Not with more glories, in th' ethereal plain,
The sun first rises o'er the purpled main,
Than, issuing forth, the rival of his beams
Launch'd on the bosom of the silver Thames.
Fair nymphs and well-dress'd youths around her shone,   5
But every eye was fix'd on her alone.
On her white breast a sparkling cross she wore,
Which Jews might kiss, and infidels adore.
Her lively looks a sprightly mind disclose,
Quick as her eyes, and as unfix'd as those: 10
Favours to none, to all she smiles extends;
Oft she rejects, but never once offends.
Bright as the sun, her eyes the gazers strike,
And, like the sun, they shine on all alike.
Yet graceful ease, and sweetness void of pride,   15
Might hide her faults, if belles had faults to hide:
If to her share some female errors fall,
Look on her face, and you'll forget them all.
    This nymph, to the destruction of mankind,
Nourish'd two locks, which graceful hung behind   20
In equal curls, and well conspired to deck
With shining ringlets the smooth ivory neck.
Love in these labyrinths his slaves detains,
And mighty hearts are held in slender chains.
With hairy springes we the birds betray,   25
Slight lines of hair surprise the finny prey,
Fair tresses man's imperial race insnare,
And beauty draws us with a single hair.
    Th' adventurous baron the bright locks admired;
He saw, he wish'd, and to the prize aspired.   30
Resolved to win, he meditates the way,
By force to ravish, or by fraud betray;
For when success a lover's toils attends,
Few ask, if fraud or force attain'd his ends.
    For this, ere Phœbus rose, he had implored   35
Propitious Heaven, and every power adored:
But chiefly Love—to Love an altar built,

Of twelve vast French romances, neatly gilt.
There lay three garters, half a pair of gloves;
And all the trophies of his former loves: 40
With tender billet-doux he lights the pyre,
And breathes three amorous sighs to raise the fire.
Then prostrate falls, and begs with ardent eyes
Soon to obtain, and long possess the prize:
The powers gave ear, and granted half his prayer,   45
The rest, the winds dispersed in empty air.
   But now secure the painted vessel glides,
The sunbeams trembling on the floating tides;
While melting music steals upon the sky,
And soften'd sounds along the waters die;   50
Smooth flow the waves, the zephyrs gently play,
Belinda smiled, and all the world was gay.
All but the sylph—with careful thoughts oppress'd,
Th' impending woe sat heavy on his breast.
He summons straight his denizens of air;   55
The lucid squadrons round the sails repair:
Soft o'er the shrouds aërial whispers breathe,
That seem'd but zephyrs to the train beneath.
Some to the sun their insect-wings unfold,
Waft on the breeze, or sink in clouds of gold;   60
Transparent forms, too fine for mortal sight,
Their fluid bodies half dissolved in light.
Loose to the wind their airy garments flew,
Thin glittering textures of the filmy dew,
Dipp'd in the richest tincture of the skies,   65
Where light disports in ever-mingling dyes;
While ev'ry beam new transient colours flings,
Colours that change whene'er they wave their wings.
Amid the circle on the gilded mast,
Superior by the head, was Ariel placed;   70
His purple pinions op'ning to the sun,
He raised his azure wand, and thus begun:
  'Ye sylphs and sylphids, to your chief give ear;
Fays, fairies, genii, elves, and dæmons, hear:
Ye know the spheres, and various tasks assign'd   75
By laws eternal to the aërial kind.
Some in the fields of purest ether play,
And bask and whiten in the blaze of day.
Some guide the course of wand'ring orbs on high,
Or roll the planets through the boundless sky.   80
Some less refined beneath the moon's pale light
Pursue the stars that shoot athwart the night,
Or suck the mists in grosser air below,
Or dip their pinions in the painted bow,
Or brew fierce tempests on the wintry main,   85

Or o'er the glebe distil the kindly rain.
Others on earth o'er human race preside,
Watch all their ways, and all their actions guide:
Of these the chief the care of nations own,
And guard with arms divine the British throne.   90
   'Our humbler province is to tend the fair,
Not a less pleasing, though less glorious care;
To save the powder from too rude a gale,
Nor let the imprison'd essences exhale;
To draw fresh colours from the vernal flowers;   95
To steal from rainbows, ere they drop in showers,
A brighter wash; to curl their waving hairs,
Assist their blushes and inspire their airs;
Nay, oft, in dreams, invention we bestow,
To change a flounce, or add a furbelow.   100
   'This day, black omens threat the brightest fair
That e'er deserved a watchful spirit's care;
Some dire disaster, or by force, or flight;
But what, or where, the Fates have wrapp'd in night.
Whether the nymph shall break Diana's law,   105
Or some frail china-jar receive a flaw;
Or stain her honour or her new brocade;
Forget her prayers, or miss a masquerade;
Or lose her heart, or necklace, at a ball;
Or whether Heaven has doom'd that Shock must fall.   110
Haste, then, ye spirits! to your charge repair:
The flutt'ring fan be Zephyretta's care;
The drops to thee, Brillante, we consign;
And, Momentilla, let the watch be thine;
Do thou, Crispissa, tend her fav'rite lock;   115
Ariel himself shall be the guard of Shock.
   'To fifty chosen sylphs, of special note,
We trust th' important charge, the petticoat:
Oft have we known that seven-fold fence to fail,
Though stiff with hoops, and arm'd with ribs of whale;   120
Form a strong line about the silver bound,
And guard the wide circumference around.
   'Whatever spirit, careless of his charge,
His post neglects, or leaves the fair at large,
Shall feel sharp vengeance soon o'ertake his sins,   125
Be stopp'd in vials, or transfix'd with pins;
Or plunged in lakes of bitter washes lie,
Or wedged whole ages in a bodkin's eye:
Gums and pomatums shall his flight restrain,
While clogg'd he beats his silken wings in vain: 130
Or alum styptics with contracting power
Shrink his thin essence like a rivell'd flower:
Or, as Ixion fix'd, the wretch shall feel

The giddy motion of the whirling wheel,
In fumes of burning chocolate shall glow,   135
And tremble at the sea that froths below!'
   He spoke; the spirits from the sails descend;
Some, orb in orb, around the nymph extend;
Some thrid the mazy ringlets of her hair;
Some hang upon the pendants of her ear: 140
With beating hearts the dire event they wait,
Anxious and trembling for the birth of Fate.

Canto III

Close by those meads, for ever crown'd with flowers,
Where Thames with pride surveys his rising towers,
There stands a structure of majestic frame,
Which from the neighb'ring Hampton takes its name.
Here Britain's statesmen oft the fall foredoom   5
Of foreign tyrants, and of nymphs at home;
Here thou, great ANNA! whom three realms obey,
Dost sometimes counsel take—and sometimes tea.
   Hither the heroes and the nymphs resort,
To taste a while the pleasures of a court;   10
In various talk th' instructive hours they pass'd,
Who gave the ball, or paid the visit last;
One speaks the glory of the British Queen,
And one describes a charming Indian screen;
A third interprets motions, looks, and eyes;   15
At every word a reputation dies.
Snuff, or the fan, supply each pause of chat,
With singing, laughing, ogling, *and all that.*
   Meanwhile, declining from the noon of day,
The sun obliquely shoots his burning ray;   20
The hungry judges soon the sentence sign,
And wretches hang that jurymen may dine;
The merchant from th' exchange returns in peace,
And the long labours of the toilet cease.
Belinda now, whom thirst of fame invites,   25
Burns to encounter two adventurous knights,
At ombre singly to decide their doom;
And swells her breast with conquests yet to come.
Straight the three bands prepare in arms to join,
Each band the number of the sacred nine.   30
Soon as she spreads her hand, th' aërial guard
Descend, and sit on each important card:
First Ariel perch'd upon a Matadore,
Then each according to the rank he bore;
For sylphs, yet mindful of their ancient race,   35

Are, as when women, wondrous fond of place.
    Behold, four Kings in majesty revered,
With hoary whiskers and a forky beard;
And four fair Queens, whose hands sustain a flower,
Th' expressive emblem of their softer power;   40
Four knaves in garbs succinct, a trusty band;
Caps on their heads, and halberts in their hand;
And party-colour'd troops, a shining train,
Drawn forth to combat on the velvet plain.
    The skilful nymph reviews her force with care: 45
'Let Spades be trumps!' she said, and trumps they were.
    Now move to war her sable Matadores,
In show like leaders of the swarthy Moors.
Spadillio first, unconquerable lord!
Led off two captive trumps, and swept the board.   50
As many more Manillio forced to yield,
And march'd a victor from the verdant field.
Him Basto follow'd; but his fate more hard
Gain'd but one trump, and one plebeian card.
With his broad sabre next, a chief in years,   55
The hoary Majesty of Spades appears,
Puts forth one manly leg, to sight reveal'd,
The rest, his many-colour'd robe conceal'd.
The rebel Knave, who dares his prince engage,
Proves the just victim of his royal rage.   60
Ev'n mighty Pam, that kings and queens o'erthrew,
And mow'd down armies in the fights of Lu,
Sad chance of war! now destitute of aid,
Falls undistinguish'd by the victor Spade!
    Thus far both armies to Belinda yield;   65
Now to the baron fate inclines the field.
His warlike Amazon her host invades,
Th' imperial consort of the crown of Spades.
The Club's black tyrant first her victim dyed,
Spite of his haughty mien, and barb'rous pride: 70
What boots the regal circle on his head,
His giant limbs, in state unwieldy spread;
That long behind he trails his pompous robe,
And, of all monarchs, only grasps the globe?
    The baron now his Diamonds pours apace;   75
Th' embroider'd King who shows but half his face,
And his refulgent Queen, with powers combined
Of broken troops an easy conquest find.
Clubs, Diamonds, Hearts, in wild disorder seen,
With throngs promiscuous strow the level green.   80
Thus when dispersed a routed army runs,
Of Asia's troops, and Afric's sable sons,
With like confusion different nations fly,

Of various habit, and of various dye,
The pierced battalions disunited fall,   85
In heaps on heaps; one fate o'erwhelms them all.
   The Knave of Diamonds tries his wily arts,
And wins (oh shameful chance!) the Queen of Hearts.
At this, the blood the virgin's cheek forsook,
A livid paleness spreads o'er all her look;   90
She sees, and trembles at th' approaching ill,
Just in the jaws of ruin, and Codille.
And now (as oft in some distemper'd state)
On one nice trick depends the gen'ral fate,
An Ace of Hearts steps forth: the King unseen   95
Lurk'd in her hand, and mourn'd his captive Queen:
He springs to vengeance with an eager pace,
And falls like thunder on the prostrate Ace.
The nymph exulting fills with shouts the sky;
The walls, the woods, and long canals reply.   100
   O thoughtless mortals! ever blind to fate,
Too soon dejected, and too soon elate.
Sudden, these honours shall be snatch'd away,
And cursed for ever this victorious day.
   For lo! the board with cups and spoons is crown'd,   105
The berries crackle, and the mill turns round:
On shining altars of Japan they raise
The silver lamp; the fiery spirits blaze:
From silver spouts the grateful liquors glide,
While China's earth receives the smoking tide: 110
At once they gratify their scent and taste,
And frequent cups prolong the rich repast.
Straight hover round the fair her airy band;
Some, as she sipp'd, the fuming liquor fann'd,
Some o'er her lap their careful plumes display'd,   115
Trembling, and conscious of the rich brocade.
Coffee (which makes the politician wise,
And see through all things with his half-shut eyes)
Sent up in vapours to the baron's brain
New stratagems, the radiant lock to gain.   120
Ah cease, rash youth! desist ere 'tis too late,
Fear the just gods, and think of Scylla's fate!
Changed to a bird, and sent to flit in air,
She dearly pays for Nisus' injured hair!
   But when to mischief mortals bend their will,   125
How soon they find fit instruments of ill!
Just then, Clarissa drew with tempting grace
A two-edged weapon from her shining case:
So ladies, in romance, assist their knight,
Present the spear, and arm him for the fight.   130
He takes the gift with reverence and extends

The little engine on his fingers' ends;
This just behind Belinda's neck he spread,
As o'er the fragrant steams she bends her head.
Swift to the lock a thousand sprites repair,   135
A thousand wings, by turns, blow back the hair;
And thrice they twitch'd the diamond in her ear;
Thrice she look'd back, and thrice the foe drew near.
Just in that instant, anxious Ariel sought
The close recesses of the virgin's thought: 140
As on the nosegay in her breast reclin'd,
He watch'd th' ideas rising in her mind,
Sudden he view'd, in spite of all her art,
An earthly lover lurking at her heart.
Amazed, confused, he found his power expired,   145
Resign'd to fate, and with a sigh retired.
The peer now spreads the glitt'ring forfex wide,
T' inclose the lock; now joins it, to divide.
Ev'n then, before the fatal engine closed,
A wretched sylph too fondly interposed;   150
Fate urged the shears, and cut the sylph in twain,
(But airy substance soon unites again)
The meeting points the sacred hair dissever
From the fair head, for ever, and for ever!
    Then flash'd the living lightning from her eyes,   155
And screams of horror rend th' affrighted skies.
Not louder shrieks to pitying Heaven are cast,
When husbands or when lap-dogs breathe their last;
Or when rich China vessels, fall'n from high,
In glitt'ring dust and painted fragments lie!   160
    'Let wreaths of triumph now my temples twine,
(The victor cried) the glorious prize is mine!
While fish in streams, or birds delight in air,
Or in a coach and six the British fair,
As long as *Atalantis* shall be read,   165
Or the small pillow grace a lady's bed,
While visits shall be paid on solemn days,
When numerous wax-lights in bright order blaze,
While nymphs take treats, or assignations give,
So long my honour, name, and praise shall live!'   170
What Time would spare, from steel receives its date,
And monuments, like men, submit to fate!
Steel could the labour of the gods destroy,
And strike to dust th' imperial towers of Troy;
Steel could the works of mortal pride confound,   175
And hew triumphal arches to the ground.
What wonder then, fair nymph! thy hairs should feel
The conquering force of unresisted steel?

Canto IV

But anxious cares the pensive nymph oppress'd,
And secret passions labour'd in her breast.
Not youthful kings in battle seized alive,
Not scornful virgins who their charms survive,
Not ardent lovers robb'd of all their bliss,   5
Not ancient ladies when refused a kiss,
Not tyrants fierce that unrepenting die,
Not Cynthia when her manteau's pinn'd awry,
E'er felt such rage, resentment, and despair,
As thou, sad virgin! for thy ravish'd hair.   10
 For, that sad moment, when the sylphs withdrew,
And Ariel weeping from Belinda flew,
Umbriel, a dusky, melancholy sprite,
As ever sullied the fair face of light,
Down to the central earth, his proper scene,   15
Repair'd to search the gloomy Cave of Spleen.
 Swift on his sooty pinions flits the gnome,
And in a vapour reach'd the dismal dome.
No cheerful breeze this sullen region knows,
The dreaded east is all the wind that blows.   20
Here in a grotto, shelter'd close from air,
And screen'd in shades from day's detested glare,
She sighs for ever on her pensive bed,
Pain at her side, and Megrim at her head.
Two handmaids wait the throne: alike in place,   25
But diff'ring far in figure and in face.
Here stood Ill-nature like an ancient maid,
Her wrinkled form in black and white array'd;
With store of prayers, for mornings, nights, and noons,
Her hand is fill'd; her bosom with lampoons.   30
 There Affectation, with a sickly mien,
Shows in her cheek the roses of eighteen,
Practised to lisp, and hang the head aside,
Faints into airs, and languishes with pride,
On the rich quilt sinks with becoming woe,   35
Wrapp'd in a gown, for sickness, and for show.
The fair ones feel such maladies as these,
When each new night-dress gives a new disease.
 A constant vapour o'er the palace flies;
Strange phantoms rising as the mists arise;   40
Dreadful, as hermits' dreams in haunted shades,
Or bright, as visions of expiring maids.
Now glaring fiends, and snakes on rolling spires,
Pale spectres, gaping tombs, and purple fires:
Now lakes of liquid gold, Elysian scenes,   45

And crystal domes, and angels in machines.
   Unnumber'd throngs on every side are seen
Of bodies changed to various forms by Spleen.
Here living tea-pots stand, one arm held out,
One bent; the handle this, and that the spout: 50
A pipkin there, like Homer's tripod walks;
Here sighs a jar, and there a goose-pie talks:
Men prove with child, as powerful fancy works,
And maids turn'd bottles call aloud for corks.
   Safe pass'd the gnome through this fantastic band,   55
A branch of healing spleen-wort in his hand.
Then thus address'd the power: 'Hail, wayward Queen!
Who rule the sex to fifty from fifteen;
Parent of vapours, and of female wit,
Who give th' hysteric or poetic fit;   60
On various tempers act by various ways,
Make some take physic, others scribble plays;
Who cause the proud their visits to delay,
And send the godly in a pet to pray;
A nymph there is, that all thy power disdains,   65
And thousands more in equal mirth maintains.
But oh! if e'er thy gnome could spoil a grace,
Or raise a pimple on a beauteous face,
Like citron waters matrons' cheeks inflame,
Or change complexions at a losing game;   70
If e'er with airy horns I planted heads,
Or rumpled petticoats, or tumbled beds,
Or caused suspicion when no soul was rude,
Or discomposed the head-dress of a prude,
Or e'er to costive lap-dog gave disease,   75
Which not the tears of brightest eyes could ease;
Hear me, and touch Belinda with chagrin,
That single act gives half the world the spleen.'
   The Goddess with a discontented air
Seems to reject him, though she grants his prayer.   80
A wondrous bag with both her hands she binds,
Like that where once Ulysses held the winds;
There she collects the force of female lungs,
Sighs, sobs, and passions, and the war of tongues.
A vial next she fills with fainting fears,   85
Soft sorrows, melting griefs, and flowing tears.
The gnome rejoicing bears her gifts away,
Spreads his black wings, and slowly mounts to day.
   Sunk in Thalestris' arms the nymph he found,
Her eyes dejected, and her hair unbound.   90
Full o'er their heads the swelling bag he rent,
And all the furies issued at the vent.
Belinda burns with more than mortal ire,

And fierce Thalestris fans the rising fire;
'O wretched maid!' she spread her hands, and cried,   95
(While Hampton's echoes, 'Wretched maid!' replied)
'Was it for this you took such constant care
The bodkin, comb, and essence to prepare?
For this your locks in paper durance bound?
For this with torturing irons wreathed around?   100
For this with fillets strain'd your tender head,
And bravely bore the double loads of lead?
Gods! shall the ravisher display your hair,
While the fops envy and the ladies stare?
Honour forbid! at whose unrivall'd shrine   105
Ease, pleasure, virtue, all, our sex resign.
Methinks already I your tears survey,
Already hear the horrid things they say,
Already see you a degraded toast,
And all your honour in a whisper lost!   110
How shall I then your helpless fame defend?
'Twill then be infamy to seem your friend!
And shall this prize, th' inestimable prize,
Exposed through crystal to the gazing eyes,
And heighten'd by the diamond's circling rays,   115
On that rapacious hand for ever blaze?
Sooner shall grass in Hyde Park Circus grow,
And wits take lodgings in the sound of Bow;
Sooner let earth, air, sea, to Chaos fall,
Men, monkeys, lap-dogs, parrots, perish all!'   120
   She said; then raging to Sir Plume repairs,
And bids her beau demand the precious hairs:
(Sir Plume of amber snuff-box justly vain,
And the nice conduct of a clouded cane)
With earnest eyes, and round, unthinking face,   125
He first the snuff-box open'd, then the case,
And then broke out—'My Lord, why, what the devil!
Zounds! damn the lock! 'fore Gad, you must be civil!
Plague on't! 'tis past a jest—nay prithee, pox!
Give her the hair'—he spoke, and rapp'd his box.   130
'It grieves me much (replied the peer again)
Who speaks so well should ever speak in vain,
But by this lock, this sacred lock, I swear,
(Which never more shall join its parted hair;
Which never more its honours shall renew,   135
Clipp'd from the lovely head where late it grew)
That while my nostrils draw the vital air,
This hand, which won it, shall for ever wear.'
He spoke, and speaking, in proud triumph spread
The long-contended honours of her head.   140
   But Umbriel, hateful gnome! forbears not so;

He breaks the vial whence the sorrows flow.
Then see! the nymph in beauteous grief appears,
Her eyes half-languishing, half-drowned in tears;
On her heaved bosom hung her drooping head,   145
Which, with a sigh, she raised; and thus she said:
  'For ever cursed be this detested day,
Which snatch'd my best, my fav'rite curl away!
Happy! ay ten times happy had I been,
If Hampton Court these eyes had never seen!   150
Yet am I not the first mistaken maid,
By love of courts to numerous ills betray'd,
Oh had I rather unadmired remain'd
In some lone isle, or distant northern land;
Where the gilt chariot never marks the way,   155
Where none learn ombre, none e'er taste bohea!
There kept my charms conceal'd from mortal eye,
Like roses that in deserts bloom and die.
What moved my mind with youthful lords to roam?
Oh had I stayed, and said my prayers at home!   160
'Twas this the morning omens seem'd to tell:
Thrice from my trembling hand the patch-box fell;
The tott'ring china shook without a wind;
Nay, Poll sat mute, and Shock was most unkind!
A sylph too warn'd me of the threats of Fate,   165
In mystic visions, now believed too late!
See the poor remnants of these slighted hairs!
My hands shall rend what e'en thy rapine spares:
These in two sable ringlets taught to break,
Once gave new beauties to the snowy neck;   170
The sister-lock now sits uncouth, alone,
And in its fellow's fate foresees its own;
Uncurl'd it hangs, the fatal shears demands,
And tempts, once more, thy sacrilegious hands.
Oh hadst thou, cruel! been content to seize   175
Hairs less in sight, or any hairs but these!'

Canto V

She said: the pitying audience melt in tears;
But Fate and Love had stopp'd the baron's ears.
In vain Thalestris with reproach assails,
For who can move when fair Belinda fails?
Not half so fix'd the Trojan could remain,   5
While Anna begg'd and Dido raged in vain.
Then grave Clarissa graceful waved her fan;
Silence ensued, and thus the nymph began:
  'Say, why are beauties praised and honoured most,

The wise man's passion, and the vain man's toast?   10
Why deck'd with all that land and sea afford?
Why angels call'd, and angel-like adored?
Why round our coaches crowd the white-gloved beaux?
Why bows the side-box from its inmost rows?
How vain are all these glories, all our pains,   15
Unless good sense preserve what beauty gains;
That men may say, when we the front-box grace,
"Behold the first in virtue as in face!"
Oh! if to dance all night, and dress all day,
Charm'd the small-pox, or chased old age away;   20
Who would not scorn what housewife's cares produce,
Or who would learn one earthly thing of use?
To patch, nay, ogle, might become a saint,
Nor could it sure be such a sin to paint.
But since, alas! frail beauty must decay,   25
Curl'd or uncurl'd, since locks will turn to grey;
Since painted, or not painted, all shall fade,
And she who scorns a man must die a maid;
What then remains, but well our power to use,
And keep good-humour still, whate'er we lose?   30
And trust me, dear, good-humour can prevail,
When airs, and flights, and screams, and scolding fail.
Beauties in vain their pretty eyes may roll;
Charms strike the sight, but merit wins the soul.'
    So spoke the dame, but no applause ensued;   35
Belinda frown'd, Thalestris call'd her prude.
'To arms, to arms!' the fierce virago cries,
And swift as lightning to the combat flies.
All side in parties, and begin th' attack:
Fans clap, silks rustle, and tough whalebones crack;   40
Heroes' and heroines' shouts confusedly rise,
And bass and treble voices strike the skies.
No common weapons in their hands are found,
Like Gods they fight, nor dread a mortal wound.
    So when bold Homer makes the gods engage,   45
And heavenly breasts with human passions rage;
'Gainst Pallas, Mars; Latona, Hermes arms;
And all Olympus rings with loud alarms;
Jove's thunder roars, Heaven trembles all around,
Blue Neptune storms, the bellowing deeps resound: 50
Earth shakes her nodding towers, the ground gives way,
And the pale ghosts start at the flash of day!
    Triumphant Umbriel on a sconce's height
Clapp'd his glad wings, and sate to view the fight:
Propp'd on their bodkin spears, the sprites survey   55
The growing combat, or assist the fray.
    While through the press enraged Thalestris flies,

And scatters death around from both her eyes,
A beau and witling perish'd in the throng,
One died in metaphor, and one in song.   60
'O cruel nymph! a living death I bear,'
Cried Dapperwit, and sunk beside his chair.
A mournful glance Sir Fopling upwards cast,
'Those eyes are made so killing,'—was his last.
Thus on Mæander's flowery margin lies   65
Th' expiring swan, and as he sings he dies.
    When bold Sir Plume had drawn Clarissa down,
Chloe stepp'd in, and kill'd him with a frown;
She smiled to see the doughty hero slain,
But, at her smile, the beau revived again.   70
    Now Jove suspends his golden scales in air,
Weighs the men's wits against the lady's hair:
The doubtful beam long nods from side to side;
At length the wits mount up, the hairs subside.
    See fierce Belinda on the baron flies,   75
With more than usual lightning in her eyes:
Nor fear'd the chief th' unequal fight to try,
Who sought no more than on his foe to die.
But this bold lord with manly strength endued,
She with one finger and a thumb subdued: 80
Just where the breath of life his nostrils drew,
A charge of snuff the wily virgin threw;
The gnomes direct, to every atom just,
The pungent grains of titillating dust.
Sudden, with starting tears each eye o'erflows,   85
And the high dome re-echoes to his nose.
    'Now meet thy fate,' incensed Belinda cried,
And drew a deadly bodkin from her side.
(The same, his ancient personage to deck,
Her great-great-grandsire wore about his neck,   90
In three seal rings; which after, melted down,
Form'd a vast buckle for his widow's gown:
Her infant grandame's whistle next it grew,
The bells she jingled, and the whistle blew;
Then in a bodkin graced her mother's hairs,   95
Which long she wore, and now Belinda wears.)
    'Boast not my fall, (he cried) insulting foe!
Thou by some other shalt be laid as low.
Nor think, to die dejects my lofty mind:
All that I dread is leaving you behind!   100
Rather than so, ah let me still survive,
And burn in Cupid's flames—but burn alive.'
    'Restore the lock!' she cries; and all around
'Restore the lock!' the vaulted roofs rebound.
Not fierce Othello in so loud a strain   105

Roar'd for the handkerchief that caused his pain.
But see how oft ambitious aims are cross'd,
And chiefs contend till all the prize is lost!
The lock, obtain'd with guilt, and kept with pain,
In every place is sought, but sought in vain: 110
With such a prize no mortal must be blest,
So Heaven decrees! with Heaven who can contest?
Some thought it mounted to the lunar sphere,
Since all things lost on earth are treasured there.
There heroes' wits are kept in pond'rous vases, 115
And beaux' in snuff-boxes and tweezer-cases.
There broken vows, and death-bed alms are found,
And lovers' hearts with ends of riband bound,
The courtier's promises, and sick man's prayers,
The smiles of harlots, and the tears of heirs, 120
Cages for gnats, and chains to yoke a flea,
Dried butterflies, and tomes of casuistry.
But trust the Muse—she saw it upward rise,
Though mark'd by none but quick, poetic eyes:
(So Rome's great founder to the heavens withdrew, 125
To Proculus alone confess'd in view)
A sudden star it shot through liquid air,
And drew behind a radiant trail of hair.
Not Berenice's lock first rose so bright,
The heavens bespangling with dishevell'd light. 130
The sylphs behold it kindling as it flies,
And pleased pursue its progress through the skies.
This the beau-monde shall from the Mall survey,
And hail with music its propitious ray.
This the blest lover shall for Venus take, 135
And send up vows from Rosamonda's lake.
This Partridge soon shall view in cloudless skies,
When next he looks through Galileo's eyes;
And hence th' egregious wizard shall foredoom
The fate of Louis, and the fall of Rome. 140
Then cease, bright nymph! to mourn thy ravish'd hair,
Which adds new glory to the shining sphere!
Not all the tresses that fair head can boast
Shall draw such envy as the lock you lost.
For, after all the murders of your eye, 145
When, after millions slain, yourself shall die;
When those fair suns shall set, as set they must,
And all those tresses shall be laid in dust;
This lock, the Muse shall consecrate to fame,
And 'midst the stars inscribe Belinda's name. 150

Eloisa to Abelard

In these deep solitudes and awful cells,
Where heavenly-pensive Contemplation dwells,
And ever-musing Melancholy reigns,
What means this tumult in a Vestal's veins?
Why rove my thoughts beyond this last retreat?   5
Why feels my heart its long-forgotten heat?
Yet, yet I love! From Abelard it came,
And Eloisa yet must kiss the name.
    Dear fatal name! rest ever unreveal'd,
Nor pass these lips in holy silence seal'd: 10
Hide it, my heart, within that close disguise,
Where, mix'd with God's, his loved idea lies:
Oh, write it not, my hand—the name appears
Already written—wash it out, my tears!
In vain lost Eloisa weeps and prays,   15
Her heart still dictates, and her hand obeys.
    Relentless walls! whose darksome round contains
Repentant sighs, and voluntary pains:
Ye rugged rocks! which holy knees have worn;
Ye grots and caverns shagg'd with horrid thorn!   20
Shrines! where their vigils pale-eyed virgins keep,
And pitying saints, whose statues learn to weep!
Though cold like you, unmoved and silent grown,
I have not yet forgot myself to stone.
All is not Heaven's while Abelard has part,   25
Still rebel nature holds out half my heart;
Nor prayers nor fasts its stubborn pulse restrain,
Nor tears for ages taught to flow in vain.
    Soon as thy letters trembling I unclose,
That well-known name awakens all my woes.   30
Oh name for ever sad! for ever dear!
Still breathed in sighs, still usher'd with a tear.
I tremble too, where'er my own I find,
Some dire misfortune follows close behind.
Line after line my gushing eyes o'erflow,   35
Led through a sad variety of woe;
Now warm in love, now with'ring in my bloom,
Lost in a convent's solitary gloom!
There stern religion quench'd th' unwilling flame,
There died the best of passions, Love and Fame.   40
    Yet write, oh write me all, that I may join
Griefs to thy grief, and echo sighs to thine.
Nor foes nor fortune take this power away;
And is my Abelard less kind than they?
Tears still are mine, and those I need not spare,   45

Love but demands what else were shed in prayer;
No happier task these faded eyes pursue;
To read and weep is all they now can do.
    Then share thy pain, allow that sad relief;
Ah, more than share it, give me all thy grief. 50
Heaven first taught letters for some wretch's aid,
Some banish'd lover, or some captive maid:
They live, they speak, they breathe what love inspires,
Warm from the soul, and faithful to its fires;
The virgin's wish without her fears impart, 55
Excuse the blush, and pour out all the heart;
Speed the soft intercourse from soul to soul,
And waft a sigh from Indus to the pole.
    Thou know'st how guiltless first I met thy flame,
When love approach'd me under friendship's name; 60
My fancy form'd thee of angelic kind,
Some emanation of th' all-beauteous mind.
Those smiling eyes, attemp'ring every ray,
Shone sweetly lambent with celestial day.
Guiltless I gazed; Heaven listen'd while you sung; 65
And truths divine came mended from that tongue.
From lips like those what precepts fail to move?
Too soon they taught me 'twas no sin to love:
Back through the paths of pleasing sense I ran,
Nor wish'd an angel whom I loved a man. 70
Dim and remote the joys of saints I see;
Nor envy them that Heaven I lose for thee.
    How oft, when press'd to marriage, have I said,
Curse on all laws but those which Love has made!
Love, free as air, at sight of human ties, 75
Spreads his light wings, and in a moment flies.
Let wealth, let honour, wait the wedded dame,
August her deed, and sacred be her fame;
Before true passion all those views remove;
Fame, wealth, and honour! what are you to love? 80
The jealous God, when we profane his fires,
Those restless passions in revenge inspires,
And bids them make mistaken mortals groan,
Who seek in love for aught but love alone.
Should at my feet the world's great master fall, 85
Himself, his throne, his world, I'd scorn them all:
Not Cæsar's empress would I deign to prove;
No, make me mistress to the man I love;
If there be yet another name more free,
More fond than mistress, make me that to thee! 90
Oh, happy state! when souls each other draw,
When love is liberty, and Nature law:
All then is full, possessing, and possessed,

No craving void left aching in the breast:
Even thought meets thought ere from the lips it part,　95
And each warm wish springs mutual from the heart.
This sure is bliss, if bliss on earth there be,
And once the lot of Abelard and me.
　　Alas, how changed! what sudden horrors rise!
A naked lover bound and bleeding lies!　100
Where, where was Eloïse? her voice, her hand,
Her poniard had opposed the dire command.
Barbarian, stay! that bloody stroke restrain;
The crime was common, common be the pain.
I can no more, by shame, by rage suppress'd　105
Let tears, and burning blushes speak the rest.
　　Canst thou forget that sad, that solemn day,
When victims at yon altar's foot we lay?
Canst thou forget what tears that moment fell,
When warm in youth I bade the world farewell?　110
As with cold lips I kiss'd the sacred veil,
The shrines all trembled, and the lamps grew pale:
Heaven scarce believed the conquest it survey'd,
And saints with wonder heard the vows I made.
Yet then, to those dread altars as I drew,　115
Not on the cross my eyes were fix'd, but you:
Not grace, or zeal, love only was my call;
And if I lose thy love, I lose my all.
Come! with thy looks, thy words, relieve my woe;
Those still at least are left thee to bestow.　120
Still on that breast enamour'd let me lie,
Still drink delicious poison from thy eye,
Pant on thy lip, and to thy heart be press'd;
Give all thou canst—and let me dream the rest.
Ah no! instruct me other joys to prize,　125
With other beauties charm my partial eyes;
Full in my view set all the bright abode,
And make my soul quit Abelard for God.
　　Ah, think at least thy flock deserves thy care,
Plants of thy hand, and children of thy prayer.　130
From the false world in early youth they fled,
By thee to mountains, wilds, and deserts led.
You raised these hallow'd walls; the desert smiled,
And Paradise was open'd in the wild.
No weeping orphan saw his father's stores　135
Our shrines irradiate, or emblaze the floors;
No silver saints by dying misers given,
Here bribed the rage of ill-required Heaven:
But such plain roofs as Piety could raise,
And only vocal with the Maker's praise.　140
In these lone walls, (their day's eternal bound)

These moss-grown domes with spiry turrets crown'd,
Where awful arches make a noon-day night,
And the dim windows shed a solemn light;
Thy eyes diffused a reconciling ray,   145
And gleams of glory brighten'd all the day.
But now no face divine contentment wears,
'Tis all blank sadness, or continual tears.
See how the force of others' prayers I try,
(O pious fraud of amorous charity!)   150
But why should I on others' prayers depend?
Come thou, my father, brother, husband, friend!
Ah, let thy handmaid, sister, daughter move,
And all those tender names in one, thy love!
The darksome pines that o'er yon rocks reclined   155
Wave high, and murmur to the hollow wind,
The wand'ring streams that shine between the hills,
The grots that echo to the tinkling rills,
The dying gales that pant upon the trees,
The lakes that quiver to the curling breeze;   160
No more these scenes my meditation aid,
Or lull to rest the visionary maid.
But o'er the twilight groves and dusky caves,
Long-sounding aisles, and intermingled graves,
Black Melancholy sits, and round her throws   165
A death-like silence, and a dread repose:
Her gloomy presence saddens all the scene,
Shades ev'ry flow'r, and darkens ev'ry green,
Deepens the murmur of the falling floods,
And breathes a browner horror on the woods.   170
    Yet here for ever, ever must I stay;
Sad proof how well a lover can obey!
Death, only death, can break the lasting chain;
And here, ev'n then, shall my cold dust remain,
Here all its frailties, all its flames resign,   175
And wait till 'tis no sin to mix with thine.
    Ah, wretch! believed the spouse of God in vain,
Confess'd within the slave of love and man.
Assist me, Heaven! but whence arose that prayer?
Sprung it from piety, or from despair?   180
Ev'n here, where frozen chastity retires,
Love finds an altar for forbidden fires.
I ought to grieve, but cannot what I ought;
I mourn the lover, not lament the fault;
I view my crime, but kindle at the view,   185
Repent old pleasures, and solicit new:
Now turn'd to Heaven, I weep my past offence,
Now think of thee, and curse my innocence.
Of all affliction taught a lover yet,

'Tis sure the hardest science to forget!   190
How shall I lose the sin, yet keep the sense,
And love the offender, yet detest th' offence?
How the dear object from the crime remove,
Or how distinguish penitence from love?
Unequal task! a passion to resign,   195
For hearts so touch'd, so pierced, so lost as mine.
Ere such a soul regains its peaceful state,
How often must it love, how often hate!
How often hope, despair, resent, regret,
Conceal, disdain,—do all things but forget!   200
But let Heaven seize it, all at once 'tis fired;
Not touch'd, but rapt; not weaken'd, but inspired!
Oh come! oh teach me nature to subdue,
Renounce my love, my life, myself—and you.
Fill my fond heart with God alone, for He   205
Alone can rival, can succeed to thee.
   How happy is the blameless Vestal's lot!
The world forgetting, by the world forgot:
Eternal sunshine of the spotless mind!
Each prayer accepted, and each wish resign'd;   210
Labour and rest that equal periods keep;
'Obedient slumbers that can wake and weep';
Desires composed, affections ever even;
Tears that delight, and sighs that waft to Heaven.
Grace shines around her with serenest beams,   215
And whispering angels prompt her golden dreams.
For her th' unfading rose of Eden blooms,
And wings of seraphs shed divine perfumes;
For her the spouse prepares the bridal ring,
For her white virgins hymeneals sing;   220
To sounds of heavenly harps she dies away,
And melts in visions of eternal day.
   Far other dreams my erring soul employ,
Far other raptures, of unholy joy:
When at the close of each sad, sorrowing day,   225
Fancy restores what vengeance snatch'd away,
Then conscience sleeps, and leaving Nature free,
All my loose soul unbounded springs to thee.
O cursed, dear horrors of all-conscious night!
How glowing guilt exalts the keen delight!   230
Provoking demons all restraint remove,
And stir within me ev'ry source of love.
I hear thee, view thee, gaze o'er all thy charms,
And round thy phantom glue my clasping arms.
I wake: — no more I hear, no more I view,   235
The phantom flies me, as unkind as you.
I call aloud; it hears not what I say:

I stretch my empty arms; it glides away.
To dream once more I close my willing eyes;
Ye soft illusions, dear deceits, arise!   240
Alas, no more! methinks we wand'ring go
Through dreary wastes, and weep each other's woe,
Where round some mould'ring tower pale ivy creeps,
And low-brow'd rocks hang nodding o'er the deeps.
Sudden you mount, you beckon from the skies;   245
Clouds interpose, waves roar, and winds arise.
I shriek, start up, the same sad prospect find,
And wake to all the griefs I left behind.
    For thee the Fates, severely kind, ordain
A cool suspense from pleasure and from pain;   250
Thy life a long dead calm of fix'd repose;
No pulse that riots, and no blood that glows.
Still as the sea, ere winds were taught to blow,
Or moving spirit bade the waters flow;
Soft as the slumbers of a saint forgiven,   255
And mild as opening gleams of promised Heaven.
    Come, Abelard! for what hast thou to dread?
The torch of Venus burns not for the dead.
Nature stands check'd; religion disapproves:
Ev'n thou art cold—yet Eloïsa loves.   260
Ah hopeless, lasting flames! like those that burn
To light the dead, and warm th' unfruitful urn.
    What scenes appear where'er I turn my view?
The dear ideas, where I fly, pursue,
Rise in the grove, before the altar rise,   265
Stain all my soul, and wanton in my eyes.
I waste the matin lamp in sighs for thee,
Thy image steals between my God and me,
Thy voice I seem in ev'ry hymn to hear,
With ev'ry bead I drop too soft a tear.   270
When from the censer clouds of fragrance roll,
And swelling organs lift the rising soul,
One thought of thee puts all the pomp to flight,
Priests, tapers, temples, swim before my sight:
In seas of flame my plunging soul is drowned,   275
While altars blaze, and angels tremble round.
    While prostrate here in humble grief I lie,
Kind, virtuous drops just gath'ring in my eye,
While praying, trembling, in the dust I roll,
And dawning grace is opening on my soul: 280
Come, if thou dar'st, all charming as thou art!
Oppose thyself to Heaven; dispute my heart;
Come, with one glance of those deluding eyes
Blot out each bright idea of the skies;
Take back that grace, those sorrows, and those tears;   285

Take back my fruitless penitence and prayers;
Snatch me, just mounting, from the bless'd abode;
Assist the fiends and tear me from my God!
  No, fly me, fly me, far as pole from pole;
Rise Alps between us! and whole oceans roll!   290
Ah, come not, write not, think not once of me,
Nor share one pang of all I felt for thee,
Thy oaths I quit, thy memory resign;
Forget, renounce me, hate whate'er was mine.
Fair eyes, and tempting looks, (which yet I view!)   295
Long loved, adored ideas, all adieu!
O Grace serene! O Virtue heavenly fair!
Divine oblivion of low-thoughted care!
Fresh blooming Hope, gay daughter of the sky!
And Faith, our early immortality!   300
Enter, each mild, each amicable guest:
Receive, and wrap me in eternal rest!
  See in her cell sad Eloïsa spread,
Propped on some tomb, a neighbour of the dead.
In each low wind methinks a spirit calls,   305
And more than echoes talk along the walls.
Here, as I watch'd the dying lamps around,
From yonder shrine I heard a hollow sound.
'Come, sister, come! (it said, or seem'd to say,)
Thy place is here, sad sister, come away!   310
Once, like thyself, I trembled, wept, and prayed,
Love's victim then, though now a sainted maid:
But all is calm in this eternal sleep;
Here Grief forgets to groan, and Love to weep,
Ev'n Superstition loses ev'ry fear: 315
For God, not man, absolves our frailties here.'
I come, I come! prepare your roseate bowers,
Celestial palms, and ever-blooming flowers.
Thither, where sinners may have rest, I go,
Where flames refined in breasts seraphic glow: 320
Thou, Abelard! the last sad office pay,
And smooth my passage to the realms of day;
See my lips tremble, and my eyeballs roll,
Suck my last breath, and catch my flying soul!
Ah no—in sacred vestments may'st thou stand,   325
The hallow'd taper trembling in thy hand,
Present the cross before my lifted eye,
Teach me at once, and learn of me to die.
Ah then, thy once-loved Eloïsa see!
It will be then no crime to gaze on me.   330
See from my cheek the transient roses fly!
See the last sparkle languish in my eye!
Till ev'ry motion, pulse, and breath be o'er,

And ev'n my Abelard be lov'd no more.
O Death all-eloquent! you only prove   335
What dust we dote on, when 'tis man we love.
   Then too, when fate shall thy fair frame destroy
(That cause of all my guilt, and all my joy),
In trance ecstatic may thy pangs be drown'd,
Bright clouds descend, and angels watch thee round;   340
From opening skies may streaming glories shine,
And saints embrace thee with a love like mine.
   May one kind grave unite each hapless name,
And graft my love immortal on thy fame!
Then, ages hence, when all my woes are o'er,   345
When this rebellious heart shall beat no more;
If ever chance two wand'ring lovers brings
To Paraclete's white walls and silver springs,
O'er the pale marble shall they join their heads,
And drink the falling tears each other sheds;   350
Then sadly say, with mutual pity moved,
'Oh may we never love as these have loved!'
From the full choir when loud Hosannas rise,
And swell the pomp of dreadful sacrifice,
Amid that scene, if some relenting eye   355
Glance on the stone where our cold relics lie,
Devotion's self shall steal a thought from Heaven,
One human tear shall drop, and be forgiven.
And sure, if Fate some future bard shall join,
In sad similitude of griefs to mine,   360
Condemn'd whole years in absence to deplore,
And image charms he must behold no more;
Such if there be, who love so long, so well,
Let him our sad, our tender story tell;
The well-sung woes will soothe my pensive ghost;   365
He best can paint them who shall feel them most.

Elegy to the Memory of an Unfortunate Lady

What beckoning ghost along the moonlight shade
Invites my steps, and points to yonder glade?
'Tis she!—but why that bleeding bosom gored,
Why dimly gleams the visionary sword?
Oh, ever beauteous, ever friendly! tell,   5
Is it, in heaven, a crime to love too well?
To bear too tender or too firm a heart,
To act a lover's or a Roman's part?
Is there no bright reversion in the sky
For those who greatly think, or bravely die?   10
   Why bade ye else, ye powers! her soul aspire

Above the vulgar flight of low desire?
Ambition first sprung from your blest abodes,
The glorious fault of angels and of gods:
Thence to their images on earth it flows,   15
And in the breast of kings and heroes glows.
Most souls, 'tis true, but peep out once an age,
Dull, sullen prisoners in the body's cage:
Dim lights of life, that burn a length of years,
Useless, unseen, as lamps in sepulchres;   20
Like Eastern kings a lazy state they keep,
And, close confined to their own palace, sleep.
   From these perhaps (ere Nature bade her die)
Fate snatched her early to the pitying sky.
As into air the purer spirits flow,   25
And separate from their kindred dregs below;
So flew the soul to its congenial place,
Nor left one virtue to redeem her race.
   But thou, false guardian of a charge too good,
Thou, mean deserter of thy brother's blood!   30
See on these ruby lips the trembling breath,
These cheeks now fading at the blast of death;
Cold is that breast which warm'd the world before,
And those love-darting eyes must roll no more.
Thus, if eternal justice rules the ball,   35
Thus shall your wives, and thus your children fall:
On all the line a sudden vengeance waits,
And frequent hearses shall besiege your gates;
There passengers shall stand, and pointing say
(While the long funerals blacken all the way),   40
'Lo! these were they, whose souls the Furies steel'd,
And cursed with hearts unknowing how to yield.'
Thus unlamented pass the proud away,
The gaze of fools, and pageant of a day!
So perish all, whose breast ne'er learn'd to glow   45
For others' good, or melt at others' woe.
   What can atone (oh ever-injured shade!)
Thy fate unpitied, and thy rites unpaid?
No friend's complaint, no kind domestic tear
Pleased thy pale ghost, or graced thy mournful bier.   50
By foreign hands thy dying eyes were closed,
By foreign hands thy decent limbs composed,
By foreign hands thy humble grave adorn'd,
By strangers honour'd, and by strangers mourn'd!
What, though no friends in sable weeds appear,   55
Grieve for an hour, perhaps then mourn a year,
And bear about the mockery of woe
To midnight dances, and the public show?
What, though no weeping loves thy ashes grace,

Nor polish'd marble emulate thy face?   60
What, though no sacred earth allow thee room,
Nor hallow'd dirge be mutter'd o'er thy tomb?
Yet shall thy grave with rising flowers be dress'd,
And the green turf lie lightly on thy breast:
There shall the morn her earliest tears bestow,   65
There the first roses of the year shall blow;
While angels with their silver wings o'ershade
The ground now sacred by thy reliques made.
   So peaceful rests, without a stone, a name,
What once had beauty, titles, wealth, and fame.   70
How loved, how honour'd once, avails thee not,
To whom related, or by whom begot;
A heap of dust alone remains of thee,
'Tis all thou art, and all the proud shall be!
   Poets themselves must fall, like those they sung,   75
Deaf the praised ear, and mute the tuneful tongue.
Even he, whose soul now melts in mournful lays,
Shall shortly want the generous tear he pays;
Then from his closing eyes thy form shall part,
And the last pang shall tear thee from his heart,   80
Life's idle business at one gasp be o'er,
The Muse forgot, and thou beloved no more!

Samuel Johnson
(1709–1784)

The Vanity of Human Wishes

The Tenth Satire of Juvenal, Imitated

Let Observation with extensive View,
Survey Mankind, from *China* to *Peru*;
Remark each anxious Toil, each eager Strife,
And watch the busy Scenes of crowded Life;
Then say how Hope and Fear, Desire and Hate,   5
O'erspread with Snares the clouded Maze of Fate,
Where wav'ring Man, betrayed by vent'rous Pride,
To tread the dreary Paths without a Guide;
As treach'rous Phantoms in the Mist delude,
Shuns fancied Ills, or chases airy Good.   10
How rarely Reason guides the stubborn Choice,
Rules the bold Hand, or prompts the suppliant Voice,
How Nations sink, by darling Schemes oppressed,
When Vengeance listens to the Fool's Request.
Fate wings with every Wish th' afflictive Dart,   15
Each Gift of Nature, and each Grace of Art,
With fatal Heat impetuous Courage glows,
With fatal Sweetness Elocution flows,
Impeachment stops the Speaker's pow'rful Breath,
And restless Fire precipitates on Death.   20
   But scarce observed the Knowing and the Bold,
Fall in the gen'ral Massacre of Gold;
Wide-wasting Pest! that rages unconfined,
And crowds with Crimes the Records of Mankind,
For Gold his Sword the Hireling Ruffian draws,   25
For Gold the hireling Judge distorts the Laws;
Wealth heaped on wealth, nor Truth nor Safety buys,
The Dangers gather as the Treasures rise.
   Let Hist'ry tell where rival Kings command,
And dubious Title shakes the madded Land,   30
When Statutes glean the Refuse of the Sword,
How much more safe the Vassal than the Lord,
Low skulks the Hind beneath the Rage of Pow'r,
And leaves the *bonny Traitor* in the *Tow'r*,

Untouched his Cottage, and his Slumbers sound,   35
Though Confiscation's Vultures clang around.
   The needy Traveller, serene and gay,
Walks the wild Heath, and sings his Toil away.
Does Envy seize thee? crush th' upbraiding Joy,
Increase his Riches and his Peace destroy;   40
Now Fears in dire Vicissitude invade,
The rustling Brake alarms, and quiv'ring Shade,
Nor Light nor Darkness bring his Pain Relief,
One shows the Plunder, and one hides the Thief.
   Yet still one gen'ral Cry the Skies assails,   45
And Gain and Grandeur load the tainted Gales;
Few know the toiling Statesman's Fear or Care,
Th' insidious Rival and the gaping Heir.
   Once more, Democritus, arise on Earth,
With cheerful Wisdom and instructive Mirth,   50
See motley Life in modern Trappings dressed,
And feed with varied Fools th'eternal Jest:
Thou who couldst laugh where Want enchained Caprice,
Toil crushed Conceit, and Man was of a Piece;
Where Wealth unloved without a Mourner died,   55
And scarce a Sycophant was fed by pride;
Where ne'er was known the Form of mock Debate,
Or seen a new-made Mayor's unwieldy State;
Where change of Fav'rites made no Change of Laws,
And Senates heard before they judged a Cause;   60
How wouldst thou shake at *Britain*'s modish Tribe,
Dart the quick Taunt, and edge the piercing Gibe?
Attentive Truth and Nature to descry,
And pierce each Scene with Philosophic Eye.
To thee were solemn Toys or empty Show,   65
The Robes of Pleasure and the Veils of Woe:
All aid the Farce, and all thy Mirth maintain,
Whose Joys are causeless, or whose Griefs are vain.
   Such was the Scorn that filled the Sage's Mind,
Renewed at every Glance on Humankind;   70
How just that Scorn ere yet thy Voice declare,
Search every State, and canvass every Prayer.
   Unnumbered Suppliants crowd Preferment's Gate,
Athirst for Wealth, and burning to be great;
Delusive Fortune hears th'incessant Call,   75
They mount, they shine, evaporate, and fall.
On every Stage the Foes of Peace attend,
Hate dogs their Flight, and Insult mocks their End.
Love ends with Hope, the sinking Statesman's Door
Pours in the Morning Worshipper no more;   80
For growing Names the weekly Scribbler lies,
To growing Wealth the Dedicator flies,

From every Room descends the painted Face,
That hung the bright *Palladium* of the Place,
And smoked in Kitchens, or in Auctions sold,   85
To better Features yields the Frame of Gold;
For now no more we trace in every Line
Heroic Worth, Benevolence Divine:
The Form distorted justifies the Fall,
And Detestation rids th' indignant Wall.   90
    But will not *Britain* hear the last Appeal,
Sign her Foes' Doom, or guard her Favourites' Zeal?
Through Freedom's Sons no more Remonstrance rings,
Degrading Nobles and controlling Kings;
Our supple Tribes repress their Patriot Throats,   95
And ask no Questions but the Price of Votes;
With Weekly Libels and Septennial Ale,
Their Wish is full to riot and to rail.
    In full-blown dignity, see *Wolsey* stand,
Law in his Voice, and Fortune in his Hand: 100
To him the Church, the Realm, their Pow'rs consign,
Through him the Rays of regal Bounty shine,
Turned by his Nod the Stream of Honour flows,
His Smile alone Security bestows:
Still to new Heights his restless Wishes tow'r,   105
Claim leads to Claim, and Pow'r advances Pow'r;
Till Conquest unresisted ceased to please,
And Rights submitted, left him none to seize.
At length his Sovereign frowns – the Train of State
Mark the keen Glance, and watch the Sign to hate.   110
Where-e'er he turns he meets a Stranger's Eye,
His Suppliants scorn him, and his Followers fly;
Now drops at once the Pride of awful State,
The golden Canopy, the glitt'ring Plate,
The regal Palace, the luxurious Board,   115
The liv'ried Army, and the menial Lord.
With Age, with Cares, with Maladies oppressed,
He seeks the Refuge of Monastic Rest.
Grief aids Disease, remembered Folly stings,
And his last Sighs reproach the Faith of Kings,   120
    Speak thou, whose Thoughts at humble Peace repine,
Shall *Wolsey*'s Wealth, with *Wolsey*'s End be thine?
Or liv'st thou now, with safer Pride content,
The richest Landlord on the Banks of *Trent*?
For why did *Wolsey* by the Steps of Fate,   125
On weak Foundations raise th' enormous Weight?
Why but to sink beneath Misfortune's Blow,
With louder Ruin to the Gulfs below?
    What gave great *Villiers* to th' Assassin's Knife,
And fixed Disease on *Harley*'s closing Life?   130

What murdered *Wentworth*, and what exiled *Hyde*,
By Kings protected and to Kings allied?
What but their Wish indulged in Courts to shine,
And Pow'r too great to keep or to resign?
   When first the College Rolls receive his Name,   135
The young Enthusiast quits his Ease for Fame;
Through all his Veins the Fever of Renown,
Burns from the strong Contagion of the Gown,
O'er *Bodley*'s Dome his future Labours spread,
And *Bacon*'s Mansion trembles o'er his Head;   140
Are these thy Views? proceed, illustrious Youth,
And virtue guard thee to the Throne of Truth!
Yet should thy Soul indulge the gen'rous Heat,
Till captive Science yields her last Retreat;
Should Reason guide thee with her brightest Ray,   145
And pour on misty Doubt resistless Day;
Should no false Kindness lure to loose Delight,
Nor Praise relax, nor Difficulty fright;
Should tempting Novelty thy Cell refrain,
And Sloth effuse her Opiate Fumes in vain;   150
Should Beauty blunt on Fops her fatal Dart,
Nor claim the Triumph of a lettered Heart;
Should no Disease thy torpid Veins invade,
Nor Melancholy's Phantoms haunt thy Shade;
Yet hope not Life from Grief or Danger free,   155
Nor think the Doom of Man reversed for thee:
Deign on the passing World to turn thine Eyes,
And pause awhile from Learning, to be wise;
There mark what Ills the Scholar's Life assail,
Toil, Envy, Want, the Patron, and the Jail.   160
See Nations slowly wise, and meanly just,
To buried Merit raise the tardy Bust.
If Dreams yet flatter, once again attend,
Hear *Lydiat*'s life, and *Galileo*'s end.
   Nor deem, when Learning her last Prize bestows   165
The glitt'ring Eminence exempt from Foes;
See when the Vulgar 'scape, despised or awed,
Rebellion's vengeful Talons seize on *Laud*.
From meaner Minds, though smaller Fines content
The plundered Palace or sequestered Rent;   170
Marked out by dangerous Parts he meets the Shock,
And fatal Learning leads him to the Block:
Around his Tomb let Art and Genius weep,
But hear his Death, ye Blockheads, hear and sleep.
   The festal Blazes, the triumphal Show,   175
The ravished Standard, and the captive Foe,
The Senate's Thanks, the Gázette's pompous Tale,
With Force resistless o'er the Brave prevail.

Such Bribes the rapid *Greek* o'er *Asia* whirled
For such the steady *Romans* shook the World;   180
For such in distant Lands the *Britons* shine,
And stain with Blood the *Danube* or the *Rhine*;
This Pow'r has Praise, that Virtue scarce can warm,
Till Fame supplies the universal Charm.
Yet Reason frowns on War's unequal Game,   185
Where wasted Nations raise a single Name,
And mortgaged States their Grandsires Wreaths regret,
From Age to Age in everlasting Debt;
Wreaths which at last the dear-bought Right convey
To rust on Medals, or on Stones decay.   190
    On what Foundation stands the Warrior's Pride?
How just his Hopes let *Swedish Charles* decide;
A Frame of Adamant, a Soul of Fire,
No Dangers fright him, and no Labours tire;
O'er Love, o'er Force, extends his wide Domain,   195
Unconquered Lord of Pleasure and of Pain;
No Joys to him pacific Sceptres yield,
War sounds the Trump, he rushes to the Field;
Behold surrounding Kings their Pow'r combine,
And One capitulate, and One resign;   200
Peace courts his Hand, but spreads her Charms in vain;
'Think Nothing gained', he cries, 'till nought remain,
On *Moscow*'s Walls till *Gothic* Standards fly.
And all is Mine beneath the Polar Sky'.
The March begins in Military State,   205
And Nations on his Eye suspended wait;
Stern Famine guards the solitary Coast,
And Winter barricades the Realms of Frost;
He comes, nor Want nor Cold his Course delay; –
Hide, blushing Glory, hide *Pultowa*'s Day: 210
The vanquished Hero leaves his broken Bands,
And shows his Miseries in distant Lands;
Condemned a needy Supplicant to wait,
While Ladies interpose, and Slaves debate.
But did not Chance at length her Error mend?   215
Did no subverted Empire mark his End?
Did rival Monarchs give the fatal Wound?
Or hostile Millions press him to the Ground?
His Fall was destined to a barren Strand,
A petty Fortress, and a dubious Hand;   220
He left the Name, at which the World grew pale,
To point a Moral, or adorn a Tale.
    All Times their Scenes of pompous Woes afford,
From *Persia*'s Tyrant to *Bavaria*'s Lord.
In gay Hostility, and barb'rous Pride,   225
With half Mankind embattled at his Side,

Great *Xerxes* comes to seize the certain Prey,
And starves exhausted Regions in his Way;
Attendant Flatt'ry counts his Myriads o'er,
Till counted Myriads soothe his Pride no more;⁣ 230
Fresh Praise is tried till Madness fires his Mind,
The Waves he lashes, and enchains the Wind;
New Pow'rs are claimed, new Pow'rs are still bestowed,
Till rude Resistance lops the spreading God;
The daring *Greeks* deride the Martial Show, 235
And heap their Vallies with the gaudy Foe;
Th' insulted Sea with humbler Thoughts he gains,
A single Skiff to speed his light remains;
Th' incumbered Oar scarce leaves the dreaded Coast
Through purple Billows and a floating Host. 240
   The bold *Bavarian*, in a luckless Hour,
Tries the dread Summits of *Cesarean* Pow'r,
With unexpected Legions bursts away,
And sees defenceless Realms receive his Sway;
Short Sway! fair *Austria* spreads her mournful Charms, 245
The Queen, the Beauty, sets the World in Arms;
From Hill to Hill the Beacons rousing Blaze
Spreads wide the Hope of Plunder and of Praise;
The fierce *Croatian*, and the wild *Hussar*,
And all the Sons of Ravage crowd the War; 250
The baffled Prince in Honour's flatt'ring Bloom
Of hasty Greatness finds the fatal Doom,
His Foes' Derision, and his Subjects' Blame,
And steals to Death from Anguish and from Shame.
   Enlarge my Life with Multitude of Days, 255
In Health, in Sickness, thus the Suppliant prays;
Hides from himself his State, and shuns to know,
That Life protracted is protracted Woe.
Time hovers o'er, impatient to destroy,
And shuts up all the Passages of Joy: 260
In vain their Gifts the bounteous Seasons pour,
The Fruit Autumnal, and the Vernal Flow'r,
With listless Eyes the Dotard views the Store,
He views, and wonders that they please no more;
Now pall the tastless Meats, and joyless Wines, 265
And Luxury with Sighs her Slave resigns.
Approach, ye Minstrels, try the soothing Strain,
And yield the tuneful Lenitives of Pain:
No Sounds alas would touch th' impervious Ear,
Though dancing Mountains witnessed *Orpheus* near; 270
Nor Lute nor Lyre his feeble Pow'rs attend,
Nor sweeter Music of a virtuous Friend,
But everlasting Dictates crowd his Tongue,
Perversely grave, or positively wrong.

The still returning Tale, and ling'ring Jest,   275
Perplex the fawning Niece and pampered Guest,
While growing Hopes scarce awe the gath'ring Sneer,
And scarce a Legacy can bribe to hear;
The watchful Guests still hint the last Offence,
The Daughter's Petulance, the Son's Expense,   280
Improve his heady Rage with treach'rous Skill,
And mould his Passions till they make his Will.
     Unnumbered Maladies each Joint invade,
Lay Siege to Life and press the dire Blockade;
But unextinguished Av'rice still remains,   285
And dreaded Losses aggravate his Pains;
He turns, with anxious Heart and crippled Hands,
His Bonds of Debt, and Mortgages of Lands;
Or views his Coffers with suspicious Eyes,
Unlocks his Gold, and counts it till he dies.   290
     But grant, the Virtues of a temp'rate Prime
Bless with an Age exempt from Scorn or Crime;
An Age that melts in unperceived Decay,
And glides in modest Innocence away;
Whose peaceful Day Benevolence endears,   295
Whose Night congratulating Conscience cheers;
The gen'ral Fav'rite as the gen'ral Friend:
Such Age there is, and who could wish its End?
     Yet ev'n on this her Load Misfortune flings,
To press the weary Minutes' flagging Wings: 300
New Sorrow rises as the Day returns,
A Sister sickens, or a Daughter mourns.
Now Kindred Merit fills the sable Bier,
Now lacerated Friendship claims a Tear.
Year chases Year, Decay pursues Decay,   305
Still drops some Joy from with'ring Life away;
New Forms arise, and diff'rent Views engage,
Superfluous lags the Vet'ran on the Stage
Till pitying Nature signs the last Release,
And bids afflicted Worth retire to Peace.   310
     But few there are whom Hours like these await,
Who set unclouded in the Gulfs of Fate.
From *Lydia*'s Monarch should the Search descend,
By *Solon* cautioned to regard his End,
In Life's last Scene what Prodigies surprise,   315
Fears of the Brave, and Follies of the Wise?
From *Marlborough*'s Eyes the Streams of Dotage flow,
And *Swift* expires a Driv'ler and a Show.
     The teeming Mother, anxious for her Race,
Begs for each Birth the Fortune of a Face: 320
Yet *Vane* could tell what Ills from Beauty spring;
And *Sedley* cursed the Form that pleased a King.

Ye Nymphs of rosy Lips and radiant Eyes,
Whom Pleasure keeps too busy to be wise,
Whom Joys with soft Varieties invite   325
By Day the Frolic, and the Dance by Night,
Who frown with Vanity, who smile with Art,
And ask the latest Fashion of the Heart,
What Care, what Rules your heedless Charms shall save,
Each Nymph your Rival, and each Youth your Slave?   330
Against your Fame with Fondness Hate combines,
The Rival batters, and the Lover mines.
With distant Voice neglected Virtue calls,
Less heard, and less the faint Remonstrance falls;
Tir'd with Contempt, she quits the slipp'ry Reign,   335
And Pride and Prudence take her Seat in vain.
In crowd at once, where none the Pass defend,
The harmless Freedom, and the private Friend.
The Guardians yield, by Force superior plied;
By Int'rest, Prudence; and by Flatt'ry, Pride.   340
Here Beauty falls betrayed, despised, distressed,
And hissing Infamy proclaims the rest.
    Where then shall Hope and Fear their Objects find?
Must dull Suspense corrupt the stagnant Mind?
Must helpless Man, in Ignorance sedate,   345
Roll darkling down the Current of his Fate?
Must no Dislike alarm, no Wishes rise,
No Cries attempt the Mercies of the Skies?
Enquirer, cease, Petitions yet remain,
Which Heav'n may hear, nor deem Religion vain.   350
Still raise for Good the supplicating Voice,
But leave to Heav'n the Measure and the Choice.
Safe in his Pow'r, whose Eyes discern afar
The secret Ambush of a specious Pray'r.
Implore his Aid, in his Decisions rest,   355
Secure whate'er he gives, he gives the best.
Yet when the Sense of sacred Presence fires,
And strong Devotion to the skies aspires,
Pour forth thy Fervours for a healthful Mind,
Obedient Passions, and a Will resigned;   360
For Love, which scarce collective Man can fill;
For Patience sovereign o'er transmuted Ill;
For Faith, that panting for a happier Seat,
Counts Death kind Nature's Signal of Retreat:
These Goods for Man the Laws of Heav'n ordain,   365
These Goods he grants, who grants the Pow'r to gain;
With these celestial Wisdom calms the Mind,
And makes the Happiness she does not find.

Thomas Gray
(1716–1771)

Ode on a Distant Prospect of Eton College

Ye distant spires, ye antique towers,
That crown the watry glade,
Where grateful Science still adores
Her HENRY's holy Shade;
And ye, that from the stately brow   5
Of WINDSOR's heights th' expanse below
Of grove, of lawn, of mead survey,
Whose turf, whose shade, whose flowers among
Wanders the hoary Thames along
His silver-winding way.   10

Ah happy hills, ah pleasing shade,
Ah fields belov'd in vain,
Where once my careless childhood stray'd,
A stranger yet to pain!
I feel the gales, that from ye blow,   15
A momentary bliss bestow,
As waving fresh their gladsome wing,
My weary soul they seem to sooth,
And, redolent of joy and youth,
To breathe a second spring.   20

Say, Father THAMES, for thou hast seen
Full many a sprightly race
Disporting on thy margent green
The paths of pleasure trace,
Who foremost now delight to cleave   25
With pliant arm thy glassy wave?
The captive linnet which enthrall?
What idle progeny succeed
To chase the rolling circle's speed,
Or urge the flying ball?   30

While some on earnest business bent
Their murm'ring labours ply
'Gainst graver hours, that bring constraint

To sweeten liberty:
Some bold adventurers disdain   35
The limits of their little reign,
And unknown regions dare descry:
Still as they run they look behind,
They hear a voice in every wind,
And snatch a fearful joy.   40

  Gay hope is theirs by fancy fed,
Less pleasing when possest;
The tear forgot as soon as shed,
The sunshine of the breast:
Theirs buxom health of rosy hue,   45
Wild wit, invention ever-new,
And lively chear of vigour born;
The thoughtless day, the easy night,
The spirits pure, the slumbers light,
That fly th' approach of morn.   50

  Alas, regardless of their doom,
The little victims play!
No sense have they of ills to come,
Nor care beyond to-day:
Yet see how all around 'em wait   55
The Ministers of human fate,
And black Misfortune's baleful train!
Ah, shew them where in ambush stand
To seize their prey the murth'rous band!
Ah, tell them, they are men!   60

  These shall the fury Passions tear,
The vulturs of the mind,
Disdainful Anger, pallid Fear,
And Shame that sculks behind;
Or pineing Love shall waste their youth,   65
Or Jealousy with rankling tooth,
That inly gnaws the secret heart,
And Envy wan, and faded Care,
Grim-visag'd comfortless Despair,
And Sorrow's piercing dart.   70

  Ambition this shall tempt to rise,
Then whirl the wretch from high,
To bitter Scorn a sacrifice.
And grinning Infamy.
The stings of Falshood those shall try,   75
And hard Unkindness' alter'd eye,
That mocks the tear it forc'd to flow;
And keen Remorse with blood defil'd,

And moody Madness laughing wild
Amid severest woe.   80

   Lo, in the vale of years beneath
A griesly troop are seen,
The painful family of Death,
More hideous than their Queen:
This racks the joints, this fires the veins,   85
That every labouring sinew strains,
Those in the deeper vitals rage:
Lo, Poverty, to fill the band,
That numbs the soul with icy hand,
And slow-consuming Age.   90

   To each his suff'rings: all are men,
Condemn'd alike to groan;
The tender for another's pain,
Th' unfeeling for his own.
Yet ah! why should they know their fate?   95
Since sorrow never comes too late,
And happiness too swiftly flies.
Thought would destroy their paradise.
No more; where ignorance is bliss,
'Tis folly to be wise.   100

Sonnet [on the Death of Mr Richard West]

In vain to me the smiling Mornings shine,
And red'ning Phoebus lifts his golden Fire:
The Birds in vain their amorous descant join;
Or cheerful Fields resume their green attire:
These ears, alas! for other notes repine,   5
A different object do these eyes require.
My lonely anguish melts no heart, but mine;
And in my Breast the imperfect joys expire.
Yet Morning smiles the busy race to cheer,
And new-born Pleasure brings to happier Men: 10
The Fields to all their wonted tribute bear:
To warm their little loves the birds complain:
I fruitless mourn to him, that cannot hear,
And weep the more, because I weep in vain.

Ode on the Death of a Favourite Cat, Drowned in a Tub of Gold Fishes

'Twas on a lofty vase's side,
Where China's gayest art had dy'd

The azure flowers, that blow;
Demurest of the tabby kind,
The pensive Selima reclin'd,   5
    Gazed on the lake below.

Her conscious tail her joy declar'd;
The fair round face, the snowy beard,
    The velvet of her paws,
Her coat, that with the tortoise vies,   10
Her ears of jet, and emerald eyes,
    She saw; and purr'd applause.

Still had she gaz'd; but 'midst the tide
Two angel forms were seen to glide,
    The Genii of the stream: 15
Their scaly armour's Tyrian hue
Thro' richest purple to the view
    Betray'd a golden gleam.

The hapless Nymph with wonder saw:
A whisker first and then a claw,   20
    With many an ardent wish,
She stretch'd in vain to reach the prize.
What female heart can gold despise?
    What Cat's averse to fish?

Presumptuous Maid! with looks intent   25
Again she stretch'd, again she bent,
    Nor knew the gulf between.
(Malignant Fate sat by, and smil'd)
The slipp'ry verge her feet beguil'd,
    She tumbled headlong in.   30

Eight times emerging from the flood
She mew'd to ev'ry watry God,
    Some speedy aid to send.
No Dolphin came, no Nereid stirr'd:
Nor cruel *Tom*, nor *Susan* heard.   35
    A Fav'rite has no friend!

From hence, ye Beauties, undeceiv'd,
Know, one false step is ne'er retriev'd,
    And be with caution bold.
Not all that tempts your wand'ring eyes   40
And heedless hearts, is lawful prize;
    Nor all, that glisters, gold.

Elegy Written in a Country Church-yard

The Curfew tolls the knell of parting day,
The lowing herd wind slowly o'er the lea,
The plowman homeward plods his weary way,
And leaves the world to darkness and to me.

Now fades the glimmering landscape on the sight,   5
And all the air a solemn stillness holds,
Save where the beetle wheels his droning flight,
And drowsy tinklings lull the distant folds;

Save that from yonder ivy-mantled tow'r
The mopeing owl does to the moon complain   10
Of such, as wand'ring near her secret bow'r,
Molest her ancient solitary reign.

Beneath those rugged elms, that yew-tree's shade,
Where heaves the turf in many a mould'ring heap,
Each in his narrow cell for ever laid,   15
The rude Forefathers of the hamlet sleep.

The breezy call of incense-breathing Morn,
The swallow twitt'ring from the straw-built shed,
The cock's shrill clarion, or the echoing horn,
No more shall rouse them from their lowly bed.   20

For them no more the blazing hearth shall burn,
Or busy housewife ply her evening care:
No children run to lisp their sire's return,
Or climb his knees the envied kiss to share.

Oft did the harvest to their sickle yield,   25
Their furrow oft the stubborn glebe has broke;
How jocund did they drive their team afield!
How bow'd the woods beneath their sturdy stroke!

Let not Ambition mock their useful toil,
Their homely joys, and destiny obscure;   30
Nor Grandeur hear with a disdainful smile,
The short and simple annals of the poor.

The boast of heraldry, the pomp of pow'r,
And all that beauty, all that wealth e'er gave,
Awaits alike th' inevitable hour.   35
The paths of glory lead but to the grave.

Nor you, ye Proud, impute to These the fault,
If Mem'ry o'er their Tomb no Trophies raise,
Where thro' the long-drawn isle and fretted vault
The pealing anthem swells the note of praise.   40

Can storied urn or animated bust
Back to its mansion call the fleeting breath?
Can Honour's voice provoke the silent dust,
Or Flatt'ry sooth the dull cold ear of Death?

Perhaps in this neglected spot is laid   45
Some heart once pregnant with celestial fire;
Hands, that the rod of empire might have sway'd,
Or wak'd to extasy the living lyre.

But Knowledge to their eyes her ample page
Rich with the spoils of time did ne'er unroll;   50
Chill Penury repress'd their noble rage,
And froze the genial current of the soul.

Full many a gem of purest ray serene,
The dark unfathom'd caves of ocean bear:
Full many a flower is born to blush unseen,   55
And waste its sweetness on the desert air.

Some village-Hampden, that with dauntless breast
The little Tyrant of his fields withstood;
Some mute inglorious Milton here may rest,
Some Cromwell guiltless of his country's blood.   60

Th' applause of list'ning senates to command,
The threats of pain and ruin to despise,
To scatter plenty o'er a smiling land,
And read their history in a nation's eyes,

Their lot forbade: nor circumscrib'd alone   65
Their growing virtues, but their crimes confin'd;
Forbad to wade through slaughter to a throne,
And shut the gates of mercy on mankind,

The struggling pangs of conscious truth to hide,
To quench the blushes of ingenuous shame,   70
Or heap the shrine of Luxury and Pride
With incense kindled at the Muse's flame.

Far from the madding crowd's ignoble strife,
Their sober wishes never learn'd to stray;

Along the cool sequester'd vale of life   75
They kept the noiseless tenor of their way.

Yet ev'n these bones from insult to protect
Some frail memorial still erected nigh,
With uncouth rhimes and shapeless sculpture deck'd,
Implores the passing tribute of a sigh.   80

Their name, their years, spelt by th' unletter'd muse,
The place of fame and elegy supply:
And many a holy text around she strews,
That teach the rustic moralist to die.

For who to dumb Forgetfulness a prey,   85
This pleasing anxious being e'er resign'd,
Left the warm precincts of the chearful day,
Nor cast one longing ling'ring look behind?

On some fond breast the parting soul relies,
Some pious drops the closing eye requires;   90
Ev'n from the tomb the voice of Nature cries,
Ev'n in our Ashes live their wonted Fires.

For thee, who mindful of th' unhonour'd Dead
Dost in these lines their artless tale relate;
If chance, by lonely contemplation led,   95
Some kindred Spirit shall inquire thy fate,

Haply some hoary-headed Swain may say,
'Oft have we seen him at the peep of dawn
Brushing with hasty steps the dews away
To meet the sun upon the upland lawn.   100

There at the foot of yonder nodding beech
That wreathes its old fantastic roots so high,
His listless length at noontide would he stretch,
And pore upon the brook that babbles by.

Hard by yon wood, now smiling as in scorn,   105
Mutt'ring his wayward fancies he would rove,
Now drooping, woeful wan, like one forlorn,
Or craz'd with care, or cross'd in hopeless love.

One morn I miss'd him on the custom'd hill,
Along the heath and near his favourite tree;   110
Another came; nor yet beside the rill,
Nor up the lawn, nor at the wood was he;

The next with dirges due in sad array
Slow thro' the church-way path we saw him born.
Approach and read (for thou can'st read) the lay,   115
Grav'd on the stone beneath yon aged thorn.'

The Epitaph

Here rests his head upon the lap of Earth
A Youth to Fortune and to Fame unknown.
Fair Science frown'd not on his humble birth,
And Melancholy mark'd him for her own.   120

Large was his bounty, and his soul sincere,
Heav'n did a recompence as largely send:
He gave to Misery all he had, a tear,
He gain'd from Heav'n ('twas all he wish'd) a friend.

No farther seek his merits to disclose,   125
Or draw his frailties from their dread abode
(There they alike in trembling hope repose),
The bosom of his Father and his God.

William Collins
(1721–1759)

Ode to Fear

Thou, to whom the World unknown
With all its shadowy Shapes is shown;
Who see'st appalled th' unreal Scene
While Fancy lifts the Veil between:
   Ah *Fear*! Ah frantic *Fear*!   5
   I see, I see Thee near.
I know thy hurried Step, thy haggard Eye!
Like Thee I start, like Thee disordered fly,
For lo what *Monsters* in thy Train appear!
Danger, whose Limbs of Giant Mould   10
What mortal Eye can fixed behold?
   Who stalks his Round, an hideous Form,
Howling amidst the Midnight Storm,
Or throws him on the ridgy Steep
Of some loose hanging Rock to sleep: 15
And with him thousand Phantoms joined,
Who prompt to Deeds accursed the Mind:
And those, the Fiends, who near allied,
O'er Nature's Wounds, and Wrecks preside;
Whilst *Vengeance*, in the lurid Air,   20
Lifts her red Arm, exposed and bare:
On whom that rav'ning Brood of Fate,
Who lap the Blood of Sorrow, wait;
Who, *Fear*, this ghastly Train can see,
And look not madly wild, like Thee?   25

Epode

In earliest *Greece* to Thee with partial Choice,
   The Grief-ful Muse addressed her infant Tongue;
The Maids and Matrons, on her awful Voice,
   Silent and pale in wild Amazement hung.

Yet He the Bard who first invoked thy Name,   30
   Disdained in *Marathon* its Power to feel:

For not alone he nursed the Poet's flame,
    But reached from Virtue's Hand the Patriot's Steel.

But who is He whom later Garlands grace,
    Who left awhile o'er *Hybla*'s Dews to rove,   35
With trembling Eyes thy dreary Steps to trace,
    Where Thou and *Furies* shared the baleful Grove?

Wrapped in thy cloudy Veil th' *Incestuous Queen*
    Sighed the sad Call her Son and Husband heared,
When once alone it broke the silent Scene,   40
    And He the Wretch of *Thebes* no more appeared.

O *Fear*, I know Thee by my throbbing Heart,
    Thy withering Power inspired each mournful Line,
Though gentle *Pity* claim her mingled Part,
    Yet all the Thunders of the Scene are thine!   45

Antistrophe

Thou who such weary Lengths hast past,
Where wilt thou rest, mad Nymph, at last?
Say, wilt thou shroud in haunted Cell,
Where gloomy *Rape* and *Murder* dwell?
Or in some hollowed Seat,   50
'Gainst which the big Waves beat,
Hear drowning Sea-men's Cries in Tempests brought!
Dark Power, with shudd'ring meek submitted Thought
Be mine, to read the Visions old,
Which thy awakening Bards have told: 55
And lest thou meet my blasted View,
Hold each strange tale devoutly true;
Ne'er be I found, by Thee o'erawed,
In that thrice-hallowed Eve abroad,
When Ghosts, as Cottage-Maids believe,   60
Their pebbled Beds permitted leave,
And *Goblins* haunt from Fire, or Fen,
Or Mine, or Flood, the Walks of Men!
    O Thou whose Spirit most possessed
The sacred Seat of *Shakespeare*'s Breast!   65
But all that from thy Prophet broke,
In thy Divine Emotions spoke:
Hither again thy Fury deal,
Teach me but once like Him to feel:
His *Cypress Wreath* my Meed decree,   70
And I, O *Fear*, will dwell with *Thee!*

Ode to Evening

If aught of Oaten Stop, or Pastoral Song,
May hope, chaste *Eve*, to soothe thy modest Ear,
Like thy own solemn Springs,
Thy Springs and dying Gales,
O *Nymph* reserved, while now the bright-haired Sun   5
Sits in yon western Tent, whose cloudy Skirts,
With Brede ethereal wove,
O'erhang his wavy Bed:
Now Air is hushed, save where the weak-eyed Bat,
With short shrill Shriek, flits by on leathern Wing,   10
Or where the Beetle winds
His small but sullen Horn,
As oft he rises 'midst the twilight Path,
Against the Pilgrim borne in heedless Hum:
Now teach me, *Maid* composed,   15
To breathe some softened Strain,
Whose Numbers stealing through thy dark'ning Vale
May not unseemly with its Stillness suit,
As musing slow, I hail
Thy genial loved Return!   20
For when thy folding Star arising shows
His paly Circlet, at his warning Lamp
The fragrant *Hours*, and *Elves*
Who slept in Flowers the Day,
And many a *Nymph* who wreathes her Brows with Sedge,   25
And sheds the freshening Dew, and, lovelier still,
The *Pensive Pleasures* sweet,
Prepare thy shadowy Car.
Then lead, calm *Vot'ress*, where some sheety Lake
Cheers the lone Heath, or some time-hallowed Pile,   30
Or upland Fallows grey
Reflect its last cool Gleam.
But when chill blust'ring Winds, or driving Rain,
Forbid my willing Feet, be mine the Hut
That from the Mountain's Side   35
Views Wilds, and swelling Floods,
And Hamlets brown, and dim-discovered Spires,
And hears their simple Bell, and marks o'er all
Thy Dewy Fingers draw
The gradual dusky Veil.   40
While *Spring* shall pour his Showers, as oft he wont,
And bathe thy breathing Tresses, meekest *Eve*!
While *Summer* loves to sport
Beneath thy lingering Light;
While sallow *Autumn* fills thy Lap with Leaves;   45

Or *Winter*, yelling through the troublous Air,
Affrights thy shrinking Train,
And rudely rends thy Robes;
So long, sure-found beneath the Sylvan Shed,
Shall *Fancy, Friendship, Science*, rose-lip'd *Health*,   50
Thy gentlest Influence own,
And hymn thy favourite Name!

Oliver Goldsmith
(1730–1774)

The Deserted Village

Sweet Auburn! loveliest village of the plain,
Where health and plenty cheered the labouring swain,
Where smiling spring its earliest visit paid,
And parting summer's lingering blooms delayed:
Dear lovely bowers of innocence and ease,   5
Seats of my youth, when every sport could please,
How often have I loitered o'er thy green,
Where humble happiness endeared each scene!
How often have I paused on every charm,
The sheltered cot, the cultivated farm,   10
The never-failing brook, the busy mill,
The decent church that topped the neighbouring hill,
The hawthorn bush, with seats beneath the shade,
For talking age and whispering lovers made!
How often have I blest the coming day,   15
When toil remitting lent its turn to play,
And all the village train, from labour free,
Led up their sports beneath the spreading tree;
While many a pastime circled in the shade,
The young contending as the old surveyed;   20
And many a gambol frolicked o'er the ground,
And sleights of art and feats of strength went round;
And still, as each repeated pleasure tired,
Succeeding sports the mirthful band inspired;
The dancing pair that simply sought renown   25
By holding out to tire each other down:
The swain mistrustless of his smutted face,
While secret laughter tittered round the place;
The bashful virgin's sidelong looks of love,
The matron's glance that would those looks reprove: 30
These were thy charms, sweet village! sports like these
With sweet succession, taught e'en toil to please:
These round thy bowers their cheerful influence shed,
These were thy charms – but all these charms are fled.
    Sweet smiling village, loveliest of the lawn,   35
Thy sports are fled, and all thy charms withdrawn;

Amidst thy bowers the tyrant's hand is seen,
And desolation saddens all thy green:
One only master grasps the whole domain,
And half a tillage stints thy smiling plain.   40
No more thy glassy brook reflects the day,
But, choked with sedges, works its weedy way;
Along thy glades, a solitary guest,
The hollow-sounding bittern guards its nest;
Amidst thy desert walks the lapwing flies,   45
And tires their echoes with unvaried cries;
Sunk are thy bowers in shapeless ruin all,
And the long grass o'ertops the mould'ring wall;
And trembling, shrinking from the spoiler's hand,
Far, far away, thy children leave the land.   50
    Ill fares the land, to hastening ills a prey,
Where wealth accumulates, and men decay:
Princes and lords may flourish, or may fade;
A breath can make them, as a breath has made:
But a bold peasantry, their country's pride,   55
When once destroyed, can never be supplied.
    A time there was, ere England's griefs began,
When every rood of ground maintained its man;
For him light labour spread her wholesome store,
Just gave what life required, but gave no more: 60
His best companions, innocence and health;
And his best riches, ignorance of wealth.
    But times are altered; trade's unfeeling train
Usurp the land and dispossess the swain;
Along the lawn, where scattered hamlets rose,   65
Unwieldy wealth and cumbrous pomp repose,
And every want to opulence allied,
And every pang that folly pays to pride.
Those gentle hours that plenty bade to bloom,
Those calm desires that asked but little room,   70
Those healthful sports that graced the peaceful scene,
Lived in each look, and brightened all the green –
These, far departing, seek a kinder shore,
And rural mirth and manners are no more.
    Sweet Auburn! parent of the blissful hour,   75
Thy glades forlorn confess the tyrant's power.
Here, as I take my solitary rounds,
Amidst thy tangling walks and ruined grounds,
And, many a year elapsed, return to view
Where once the cottage stood, the hawthorn grew,   80
Remembrance wakes with all her busy train,
Swells at my breast, and turns the past to pain.
    In all my wand'rings round this world of care,
In all my griefs – and God has giv'n my share –

I still had hopes, my latest hours to crown,   85
Amidst these humble bowers to lay me down;
To husband out life's taper at the close,
And keep the flame from wasting by repose:
I still had hopes, for pride attends us still,
Amidst the swains to show my booklearned skill,   90
Around my fire an evening group to draw,
And tell of all I felt and all I saw;
And as a hare whom hounds and horns pursue,
Pants to the place from whence at first she flew,
I still had hopes, my long vexations past,   95
Here to return, and die at home at last.
   O blest retirement, friend to life's decline,
Retreats from care, that never must be mine!
How happy he who crowns in shades like these
A youth of labour with an age of ease;   100
Who quits a world where strong temptations try,
And, since 'tis hard to combat, learns to fly!
For him no wretches, born to work and weep,
Explore the mine, or tempt the dangerous deep;
No surly porter stands in guilty state,   105
To spurn imploring famine from the gate;
But on he moves to meet his latter end,
Angels around befriending virtue's friend;
Bends to the grave with unperceived decay,
While resignation gently slopes the way;   110
And, all his prospects bright'ning to the last,
His heav'n commences ere the world be past!
   Sweet was the sound, when oft at evening's close
Up yonder hill the village murmur rose.
There, as I passed with careless steps and slow,   115
The mingling notes came softened from below;
The swain responsive as the milk-maid sung,
The sober herd that lowed to meet their young,
The noisy geese that gabbled o'er the pool,
The playful children just let loose from school,   120
The watchdog's voice that bayed the whispering wind,
And the loud laugh that spoke the vacant mind, –
These all in sweet confusion sought the shade,
And filled each pause the nightingale had made.
But now the sounds of population fail,   125
No cheerful murmurs fluctuate in the gale,
No busy steps the grass-grown footway tread,
For all the bloomy flush of life is fled!
All but yon widowed, solitary thing,
That feebly bends beside the plashy spring: 130
She, wretched matron, forced in age for bread,
To strip the brook with mantling cresses spread,

To pick her wintry faggot from the thorn,
To seek her nightly shed, and weep till morn;
She only left of all the harmless train,   135
The sad historian of the pensive plain.
    Near yonder copse, where once the garden smiled,
And still where many a garden flower grows wild;
There, where a few torn shrubs the place disclose,
The village preacher's modest mansion rose.   140
A man he was to all the country dear,
And passing rich with forty pounds a year;
Remote from towns he ran his godly race,
Nor e'er had changed, nor wished to change, his place;
Unpractised he to fawn, or seek for power,   145
By doctrines fashioned to the varying hour;
Far other aims his heart had learned to prize,
More skilled to raise the wretched than to rise.
His house was known to all the vagrant train;
He chid their wanderings but relieved their pain;   150
The long remembered beggar was his guest,
Whose beard descending swept his aged breast;
The ruined spendthrift, now no longer proud,
Claimed kindred there, and had his claims allowed;
The broken soldier, kindly bade to stay,   155
Sat by his fire, and talked the night away,
Wept o'er his wounds, or, tales of sorrow done,
Shouldered his crutch and showed how fields were won.
Pleased with his guests, the good man learned to glow,
And quite forgot their vices in their woe;   160
Careless their merits or their faults to scan,
His pity gave ere charity began.
    Thus to relieve the wretched was his pride,
And e'en his failings leaned to virtue's side;
But in his duty prompt at every call,   165
He watched and wept, he prayed and felt for all;
And, as a bird each fond endearment tries
To tempt its new-fledged offspring to the skies,
He tried each art, reproved each dull delay,
Allured to brighter worlds, and led the way.   170
    Beside the bed where parting life was laid,
And sorrow, guilt, and pain, by turns dismayed
The reverend champion stood. At his control
Despair and anguish fled the struggling soul;
Comfort came down the trembling wretch to raise,   175
And his last falt'ring accents whispered praise.
    At church, with meek and unaffected grace,
His looks adorned the venerable place;
Truth from his lips prevailed with double sway,
And fools who came to scoff remained to pray.   180

The service past, around the pious man,
With steady zeal, each honest rustic ran;
E'en children followed with endearing wile,
And plucked his gown to share the good man's smile.
His ready smile a parent's warmth expressed: 185
Their welfare pleased him, and their cares distressed:
To them his heart, his love, his griefs were given,
But all his serious thoughts had rest in Heaven.
As some tall cliff that lifts its awful form,
Swells from the vale, and midway leaves the storm,   190
Though round its breast the rolling clouds are spread,
Eternal sunshine settles on its head.
  Beside yon straggling fence that skirts the way,
With blossomed furze unprofitably gay,
There, in his noisy mansion, skilled to rule,   195
The village master taught his little school.
A man severe he was, and stern to view;
I knew him well, and every truant knew;
Well had the boding tremblers learned to trace
The day's disasters in his morning face;   200
Full well they laughed with counterfeited glee
At all his jokes, for many a joke had he;
Full well the busy whisper circling round
Conveyed the dismal tidings when he frowned.
Yet he was kind, or, if severe in aught,   205
The love he bore to learning was in fault;
The village all declared how much he knew;
'Twas certain he could write, and cipher too:
Lands he could measure, terms and tides presage,
And ev'n the story ran that he could gauge.   210
In arguing, too, the parson owned his skill,
For, ev'n though vanquished, he could argue still;
While words of learned length and thundering sound
Amazed the gazing rustics ranged around;
And still they gazed, and still the wonder grew,   215
That one small head could carry all he knew.
  But past is all his fame. The very spot
Where many a time he triumphed is forgot.
Near yonder thorn, that lifts its head on high,
Where once the sign-post caught the passing eye,   220
Low lies that house where nut-brown draughts inspired,
Where greybeard mirth and smiling toil retired,
Where village statesmen talked with looks profound,
And news much older than their ale went round.
Imagination fondly stoops to trace   225
The parlour splendours of that festive place;
The whitewashed wall, the nicely-sanded floor,
The varnished clock that clicked behind the door;

The chest contrived a double debt to pay,
A bed by night, a chest of drawers by day;   230
The pictures placed for ornament and use,
The Twelve Good Rules, the Royal Game of Goose;
The hearth, except when winter chilled the day,
With aspen boughs, and flowers, and fennel gay;
While broken teacups, wisely kept for show,   235
Ranged o'er the chimney, glistened in a row.
    Vain transitory splendours! could not all
Reprieve the tottering mansion from its fall?
Obscure it sinks, nor shall it more impart
An hour's importance to the poor man's heart.   240
Thither no more the peasant shall repair
To sweet oblivion of his daily care;
No more the farmer's news, the barber's tale,
No more the woodman's ballad shall prevail;
No more the smith his dusky brow shall clear,   245
Relax his ponderous strength, and lean to hear;
The host himself no longer shall be found
Careful to see the mantling bliss go round;
Nor the coy maid, half willing to be pressed,
Shall kiss the cup to pass it to the rest.   250
    Yes! let the rich deride, the proud disdain,
These simple blessings of the lowly train;
To me more dear, congenial to my heart,
One native charm, than all the gloss of art;
Spontaneous joys, where nature has its play,   255
The soul adopts, and owns their first born sway;
Lightly they frolic o'er the vacant mind,
Unenvied, unmolested, unconfined.
But the long pomp, the midnight masquerade,
With all the freaks of wanton wealth arrayed –   260
In these, ere triflers half their wish obtain,
The toiling pleasure sickens into pain;
And, e'en while fashion's brightest arts decoy,
The heart distrusting asks if this be joy.
    Ye friends to truth, ye statesmen who survey   265
The rich man's joys increase, the poor's decay,
'Tis yours to judge, how wide the limits stand
Between a splendid and a happy land.
Proud swells the tide with loads of freighted ore,
And shouting Folly hails them from her shore;   270
Hoards e'en beyond the miser's wish abound,
And rich men flock from all the world around.
Yet count our gains. This wealth is but a name
That leaves our useful products still the same.
Not so the loss. The man of wealth and pride   275
Takes up a space that many poor supplied;

Space for his lake, his park's extended bounds,
Space for his horses, equipage, and hounds:
The robe that wraps his limbs in silken sloth
Has robbed the neighb'ring fields of half their growth: 280
His seat, where solitary sports are seen,
Indignant spurns the cottage from the green:
Around the world each needful product flies,
For all the luxuries the world supplies;
While thus the land adorned for pleasure all,   285
In barren splendour feebly waits the fall.
    As some fair female unadorned and plain,
Secure to please while youth confirms her reign,
Slights every borrowed charm that dress supplies,
Nor shares with art the triumph of her eyes;   290
But when those charms are past, for charms are frail,
When time advances, and when lovers fail,
She then shines forth, solicitous to bless,
In all the glaring impotence of dress.
Thus fares the land by luxury betrayed: 295
In nature's simplest charms at first arrayed,
But verging to decline, its splendours rise,
Its vistas strike, its palaces surprise;
While, scourged by famine from the smiling land,
The mournful peasant leads his humble band,   300
And while he sinks, without one arm to save,
The country blooms – a garden and a grave.
    Where then, ah! where, shall poverty reside,
To 'scape the pressure of contiguous pride?
If to some common's fenceless limits strayed   305
He drives his flock to pick the scanty blade,
Those fenceless fields the sons of wealth divide,
And ev'n the bare-worn common is denied.
    If to the city sped – what waits him there?
To see profusion that he must not share;   310
To see ten thousand baneful arts combined
To pamper luxury, and thin mankind;
To see those joys the sons of pleasure know
Extorted from his fellow-creature's woe.
Here while the courtier glitters in brocade,   315
There the pale artist plies the sickly trade;
Here while the proud their long-drawn pomps display,
There the black gibbet glooms beside the way.
The dome where pleasure holds her midnight reign
Here, richly decked, admits the gorgeous train: 320
Tumultuous grandeur crowds the blazing square,
The rattling chariots clash, the torches glare.
Sure scenes like these no troubles e'er annoy!
Sure these denote one universal joy!

Are these thy serious thoughts? – Ah, turn thine eyes   325
Where the poor houseless shivering female lies.
She once, perhaps, in village plenty blest,
Has wept at tales of innocence distressed;
Her modest looks the cottage might adorn
Sweet as the primrose peeps beneath the thorn: 330
Now lost to all – her friends, her virtue fled,
Near her betrayer's door she lays her head,
And, pinched with cold, and shrinking from the shower,
With heavy heart deplores that luckless hour,
When idly first, ambitious of the town,   335
She left her wheel and robes of country brown.
    Do thine, sweet Auburn, thine, the loveliest train –
Do thy fair tribes participate her pain?
Ev'n now, perhaps, by cold and hunger led,
At proud men's doors they ask a little bread!   340
    Ah, no! To distant climes, a dreary scene,
Where half the convex world intrudes between,
Through torrid tracts with fainting steps they go,
Where wild Altama murmurs to their woe.
Far different there from all that charmed before,   345
The various terrors of that horrid shore:
Those blazing suns that dart a downward ray,
And fiercely shed intolerable day;
Those matted woods, where birds forget to sing,
But silent bats in drowsy clusters cling;   350
Those poisonous fields with rank luxuriance crowned,
Where the dark scorpion gathers death around;
Where at each step the stranger fears to wake
The rattling terrors of the vengeful snake;
Where crouching tigers wait their hapless prey,   355
And savage men more murderous still than they;
While oft in whirls the mad tornado flies,
Mingling the ravaged landscape with the skies.
Far different these from every former scene,
The cooling brook, the grassy-vested green,   360
The breezy covert of the warbling grove,
That only sheltered thefts of harmless love.
    Good Heaven! what sorrows gloomed that parting day,
That called them from their native walks away;
When the poor exiles, every pleasure past,   365
Hung round their bowers, and fondly looked their last,
And took a long farewell, and wished in vain
For seats like these beyond the western main,
And shuddering still to face the distant deep,
Returned and wept, and still returned to weep!   370
The good old sire the first prepared to go
To new found worlds, and wept for others' woe;

But for himself, in conscious virtue brave,
He only wished for worlds beyond the grave.
His lovely daughter, lovelier in her tears,   375
The fond companion of his helpless years,
Silent went next, neglectful of her charms,
And left a lover's for a father's arms.
With louder plaints the mother spoke her woes,
And blessed the cot where every pleasure rose,   380
And kissed her thoughtless babes with many a tear,
And clasped them close, in sorrow doubly dear,
Whilst her fond husband strove to lend relief
In all the silent manliness of grief.
     O luxury! thou cursed by Heaven's decree,   385
How ill exchanged are things like these for thee!
How do thy potions, with insidious joy,
Diffuse their pleasures only to destroy!
Kingdoms by thee, to sickly greatness grown,
Boast of a florid vigour not their own.   390
At every draught more large and large they grow,
A bloated mass of rank unwieldy woe;
Till sapped their strength, and every part unsound,
Down, down they sink, and spread a ruin round.
     Ev'n now the devastation is begun,   395
And half the business of destruction done;
Ev'n now, methinks, as pondering here I stand,
I see the rural virtues leave the land.
Down where yon anchoring vessel spreads the sail,
That idly waiting flaps with every gale,   400
Downward they move, a melancholy band,
Pass from the shore, and darken all the strand.
Contented toil, and hospitable care,
And kind connubial tenderness, are there;
And piety, with wishes placed above,   405
And steady loyalty, and faithful love.
And thou, sweet Poetry, thou loveliest maid,
Still first to fly where sensual joys invade;
Unfit in these degenerate times of shame
To catch the heart, or strike for honest fame;   410
Dear charming nymph, neglected and decried,
My shame in crowds, my solitary pride;
Thou source of all my bliss, and all my woe,
That found'st me poor at first, and keep'st me so;
Thou guide by which the nobler arts excel,   415
Thou nurse of every virtue, fare thee well!
Farewell, and oh! where'er thy voice be tried,
On Torno's cliffs, or Pambamarca's side,
Whether where equinoctial fervours glow,
Or winter wraps the polar world in snow,   420

Still let thy voice, prevailing over time,
Redress the rigours of the inclement clime;
Aid slighted truth, with thy persuasive strain
Teach erring man to spurn the rage of gain;
Teach him that states of native strength possessed,   425
Though very poor, may still be very blest;
That trade's proud empire hastes to swift decay,
As ocean sweeps the laboured mole away;
While self-dependent power can time defy,
As rocks resist the billows and the sky.   430

Index of Titles and First Lines